THE FORBIDDEN LOVE
The Normal and Abnormal Love of Children

EDITED BY
WILLIAM KRAEMER

SHELDON PRESS
LONDON

First published in Great Britain in 1976 by
Sheldon Press, Marylebone Road, London NW1 4DU

Copyright © William Kraemer 1976

Printed in Great Britain by
Northumberland Press Limited
Gateshead

ISBN 085969 078 4

THE FORBIDDEN LOVE

Contents

Contents

Preface

The four contributors to this book are all analytical psychologists, that is, analysts of the Jungian school. Together with other Jungians and with Freudian analysts (psychoanalysts), they belong to an informal group which calls itself 'Freud Jung' and have met regularly for working suppers for more than a dozen years. The idea was conceived during an international congress in Zürich, and a few years later the group produced its first child—the Centre for the Analytical Study of Student Problems (registered as a charity).

This book is another of its children, not inappropriately a book about children—that is to say the child within ourselves and others. It is not meant for actual outer children but for the man in the street, that is 'people like you and me'. As anyone interested or involved in paedophilia must know, the subject is indeed complex. It has its roots deep in the inner world of man—a world to which poets have ready access. In exploring it in their more specialized yet also more clumsy way and in making it intelligible to themselves and others, psychotherapists have developed certain techniques and invented a vocabulary which may be a little puzzling to the outsider. To help the general reader for whom this book is primarily written, we have added at the end of the book a short glossary of the less familiar words and expressions used in the text.

All the contributors have written straight from their hearts and have given clinical illustrations of case histories to make their various points. While my colleagues have said a great deal about the process of analysis (a particular method used in psychotherapy), I have in my own chapters said almost nothing about the process itself. I hope that the different approaches to our theme will add to the liveliness of the whole for the reader.

As far as possible we have sought and obtained permission from the patients concerned to write about their cases. But it would in any case be difficult for anyone (other than the patients themselves) to guess their identity, since they have always been 'changed' sufficiently to provide a safeguard against detection.

As the editor I want particularly to thank Noel Matthews for the hard work she has done in preparing this book. Equally I want to thank my friends and fellow contributors for their patience when I have occasionally interfered with their manuscripts and hurried them towards deadlines.

Very special thanks are also due to Darley Anderson, Editor-in-Chief of Sheldon Press, who has greatly helped and frequently inspired us.

London, January 1976   **WILLIAM KRAEMER**

The Authors

WILLIAM KRAEMER, M.D., F.R.C.Psych., former Medical Director of the Davidson Clinic, Edinburgh, is an analytical psychologist who since 1957 has practised privately in London. He is a professional member of the Society of Analytical Psychology, London, Honorary Consultant of the London Marriage Guidance Council, founder member and chairman of the Centre for the Analytical Study of Student Problems (C.A.S.S.P.) and past chairman of the Medical Section of the British Psychological Society. His interest in psychology is extended to the background and dynamics of political and international affairs.

ROSEMARY GORDON, Ph.D., B.A., F.B.Ps.S., F.R.Anthrop.-Inst., is in private practice in London as an analytical psychologist and training analyst of the Society of Analytical Psychology. Past chairman of the Medical Section of the British Psychological Society and a founder member of C.A.S.S.P., her activities in the psychological field are widened by her subsidiary training in anthropology and sociology and her interest in art. She is joint editor of *The Library of Analytical Psychology.*

KENNETH LAMBERT, M.A., F.B.Ps.S., who practises as an analytical psychologist and training analyst in London and also in Cambridge, is a past chairman of the Medical Section of the British Psychological Society. He is joint editor of *The Library of Analytical Psychology* and assistant editor of the *Journal of Analytical Psychology.*

MARY WILLIAMS is a training analyst of the Society of Analytical Psychology. Former psychiatric social worker and marital therapist at the Tavistock Clinic, she is now in private practice as an analytical psychologist in London.

Apart from their professional duties, all four have contributed numerous articles on psychology and allied subjects to various journals and periodicals, including the *Journal of Analytical Psychology*, and each is the author of a section in the publication *Technique in Jungian Psychology*.

1

A Paradise Lost

William Kraemer

Thanks to the basic concepts of psychoanalysis, the importance of childhood experience has now been accepted by a wide group of psychologists, psychiatrists, physicians, sociologists and other workers in related fields. That the child is father of the man is a truism as old as mankind, but until the dawn of Freud the full implications of this old truth had not been fully explored.

A great wealth of research work has characterized the last three-quarters of a century, and the child's world is no longer unrecognized and uncharted, nor has the vital impact of this world on the development of the personality been overlooked. In analytical practice and analytically orientated psychotherapy the problem of the patient is invariably understood in the context of early events in his life; without this no interpretation is thought to be valid.

The present book is concerned with the phenomenon of paedophilia. In the past, interest has mainly focused on the forensic aspects of this subject, but we believe that it now deserves more clinical investigation, more understanding on analytical lines. Paedophilia is a frequent phenomenon in psychiatric practice, and during deep analysis paedophilic fantasies are often discovered—fantasies of which the patient had been largely or wholly unaware and which turn out to be of primary significance in his inner life. Moreover, as the theme is manifestly connected with sexual feelings, emotional longings and, no doubt, ambivalent reactions of the so-called adult towards the child figure, it seems particularly appropriate to devote time and effort to the search for a new and better assessment of the psychological antecedents and symbolic motivation which create this kind of fantasy and action.

From clinical observation it is held that the roots of paedophilic tendencies in the individual can be traced to an early situation between mother and child. A normal mother soon becomes inwardly merged with her new-born baby, as the baby does with her, and she will therefore react to him as to her own body-soul image. The stronger her natural narcissism —and a measure of narcissism is common to all of us—the greater the self-love and self-idealizing flattery she will embody in him. Owing to society's general tolerance in this respect she will be able to express a less inhibited adulation for her child than she would for her own self. Even in the present climate of freedom it is far less acceptable to praise oneself than to praise one's child, because the child is already taken to be a person in his own right, if only for this one purpose of maternal self-glorification. This glorification can also be seen in another light: it is a safeguard to keeping the mother-child figure totally good so that all badness can be projected elsewhere.

Even owls find their offspring beautiful and it can be assumed that there are few human mothers less emotionally involved with their own young than are the owls. This is an advantage for the development of the small child as his need for love and warmth is naturally very great. However, it is most important to differentiate between a mother, who sooner rather than later can *truly* accept the budding existence of a person *in his own right* and thus allow the state of intimate fusion to change gradually into a relationship between two individuals, and a mother who clings to the fusion and continues to regard the baby as part of herself or at least as her property. In the latter case the transition towards the baby's separate selfhood will be delayed. The mother-child mutual admiration society, so much desired by insecure parents, will

2

affect the attitude of the child leading to the prolonged idealization of the parent and also of *his own image*. Paradoxically this latter idealization may also be felt as a protection whenever the child's right to exist is denied him by the parent.

This state was described well by a particularly narcissistic patient with paedophilic tendencies. At the age of thirty-five he confessed to his analyst that for decades he had shared the exaggerated idea of his own beauty and charm held by his mother. Recently he had begun to find his truly beautiful and charming self which he felt—wrongly—was quite different from his mother's assessment of him. In actual fact he had now set out to create a hardly less exalted picture of his own making—something to which he was at first quite blind.

Quite often a person with this sort of background develops paedophilic interests in later life. The unconscious identification with his mother's idealized picture often goes with his own tendency to enter into a state of fusion with yet another insufficiently separate object. This amalgam retains the characteristics of his own idealized self. Such a narcissistically inflated 'so-called person' does not so much feel himself drawn towards *real* outer children as towards an imagined replica of his own self. He is fascinated by fantasy images which are superimposed on children who may themselves have very little similarity to the idealizing person or idealized figure. Hence this image remains the exclusive inner property of its projector.

Looked at in another way, however, it is nobody's property. That is why the projector was referred to as a 'so-called person' (and similarly I referred earlier to a 'so-called adult'). This is because we are not dealing here with an individual in the true sense of the word, still less with 'an adult'. The projector must be understood first as a passive receiver of an impulse and secondly as an active reactor. Someone who, as it were, receives the message and acts on it in a mechanical way. Whenever this mode of reaction characterizes behaviour and conscious and deliberate purpose is absent, we are seeing events which

3

are subject to collective drives and contents. The more this applies to a given situation the less appropriate is the euphemism 'adult' and the less justification there is for talking about a *person*. For a real person would be more or less a free agent with a considerable degree of choice of action at his disposal.

Such autonomous events then are of an impersonal nature. The person is subject to archetypal influence and dominance and is not, relatively speaking, his own master. This is not to be taken as a medical description of reduced responsibility, although such a description might well apply to an acting-out paedophil. What must be emphasized is the essentially different dimension of such an event—namely its relatedness to the collective unconscious. This becomes increasingly obvious the more insight we gain into the *impersonal* nature of the feelings which dominate the so-called adult lover of young boys or girls. The following example of a typical case of paedophilia illustrates this important fact.

The patient is a man of intelligence and ability in his late twenties, with a pronounced maternal fusion and an absent father as his background. He described his feelings in the following way:

The children I am drawn to are usually very pretty. They invariably remind me of myself as a child, or if they are not actually like me they are certainly what I could have been like if my childhood circumstances had been different and if I had been less shy. I have had sexual dealings with a considerable number of such kids, and while it was always very sad to lose the particular little lover, who for a few short hours or sometimes even days or weeks was the inspirer of my feverish dreams and actions, the loss hardly ever led to any painful grieving for more than a short while —a matter of hours rather than days. The very first incident, however, was different. I was just under twenty when I lost my little twelve-year-old darling and I was quite desperate and on the verge of suicide. He remained the prototype of all the children I have loved since, but they have all proved

4

to be replaceable to an unbelievable degree. I feel very deeply about each one of them but they count less as separate people and all seem to have the same essential lovability in common. They are all equal in beauty and responsiveness. I am a lucky person to have this particular desire because wherever I go there will always be new children and they will always be ready to love my body and admire me just as I am ready to give them all they could possibly want in a relationship.

The psychologist Jung gave pride of place to some of the archetypes of the Collective or Impersonal Unconscious, and in keeping with the Christ-child tradition he saw the divine child as one of the most meaningful and dynamic leaders of man's soul. Although the emphasis on the baby Jesus precludes overt sexual fantasies, the twelve-year-old saviour teaching his elders in the Temple could have been an inspirer in more than one sense. Goethe is reported to have written a doggerel referring to the Christ boy's penis, but if such a doggerel exists it is not to be found in the Collected Works, however much it belongs to the Collective Unconscious.

It is doubtful whether the paedophil is really justified in speaking of his 'goings-on' with children as a relationship. Is this not a dream fusion, such as one can fantasy with the gods, and the gods only? The fantasy often corresponds closely to that held by the young child and the conspiring mother in the early idealized position. It is indeed typical for paedophils to see themselves at times in the role of the admired phallus carrier and then again as the admiring parent-lover.

A further clinical example illustrates this. A man in his early twenties gave the following account of his sex ploys with pre-adolescent boys.

Usually we take turns in admiring each other's penis. His is small and graceful, and I have the power to make it stiff by kissing and fondling it. The boy is a little apprehensive at first, but soon he trusts me sufficiently to let me do what I

5

like. He often becomes very withdrawn, with his eyes shut, sucking his thumb and apparently hardly aware of me. He is in some kind of trance and once he comes back to life after some sort of orgasm he doesn't want me to go on with the game. It is often quite difficult to persuade him to do the same to me, because of course I am very excited by this time and rather greedy. I show him my penis and make him hold it, and then I may even succeed in being masturbated by him. More often than not he is rather bored by this part and they (the boys) are rather inclined to talk about other things which have nothing to do with me. As long as they pay tribute to the size of my penis, even if they add that it doesn't appeal to them, I am satisfied and it doesn't matter much whether they masturbate me to the end or lose interest and have me finish it off by myself.

This more or less verbatim account re-emphasizes some previously made points. The transition from singular to plural—from the boy to the boys—speaks for itself. The somewhat ritualistic procedure described by the patient again bears witness to the impersonal nature of the whole matter. Even though the fusion characteristic is *apparently* lacking in this instance, the fact is that—as in the case of fusion—one of the *participants* seems to disappear and only one remains. They take turns in disappearing as it were, since in the second part of the rite it is the paedophil who really withdraws from the boy and concentrates on his own masturbatory images, although one has to read this between the lines as it is not explicitly stated. There is no question of a duet between two lovers, because there aren't two lovers. In fact, as a ritualistic, collective event there is not even one lover present. Only the gods are there—Cupid and Zeus—egocentric and not relating, as neither participant exists for the other in outer reality. However, this is only one aspect of the paedophilic event.

The poetic element in the paedophil story cannot be simply dismissed: the adult's love for boys and girls is second only in importance to love between man and woman, as is evident from the volume and quality of paedophilic poetry and prose. It is precisely because of its frequently much idealized and largely unreal character that child love lends itself to literary perfection, at least of the troubadour, ivory tower kind. 'It is all in the mind,' as a paedophil defendant once declared in court to the astonished judge. 'That is not how it looks to me,' the judge retorted and requested an explanation. 'Well, my lord,' the other replied, 'my love for these boys is of a highly spiritual nature however crude and physical it might sound to the outsider. That is what I meant.'

The man in the dock had, of course, made a poetic statement which bears the mark of truth. In ancient Greece and Rome everyone would have recognized it, because the concept of the beautiful and good was deeply ingrained in these ancient cultures and the paedophil of those days would not in any case have found himself in the dock.

Today the man in the street, even in our enlightened democracy, would shrug his shoulders and call the defendant a hypocrite. Most would not believe him or even listen to him, and seventy-five per cent of the signatories of an imagined correspondence in *The Times* would express their disbelief too. It is also noticeable how intolerant other groups of sexual deviants are towards this particular group. Many homosexuals, for instance, express indignation or moral disapproval of paedophils, who are an easy target for moralistic judgement and hurtful mockery. Viewing this common antipathy in its most positive way it could be seen as the expression of an unconscious general suspicion of idealization. One might, for instance, credit the man in the street with an inherent knowledge that it is blasphemous to make love to the angels (i.e. archetypes), for which sin the city of Sodom was reputedly annihilated by the Lord God. However, it is more likely that a great deal of unconscious envy motivates this widespread condemnation by society. Such is the fear of commitment in a true relationship that anyone who can 'get away with it' and get pleasure and sexual gratification without commitment is felt to have an unfair advantage over the rest of us. Like the fowls of the air they

7

sow not neither do they reap, yet our Heavenly Father nourishes them with good things.

The major source of confusion is over the meaning of the word 'spiritual'. In its nineteenth-century context, which is still prevalent in many a Sunday pulpit, it was synonymous with 'divine' and was personified by the Third Person of the Trinity. On the other hand the idea of evil spirits has also been accepted since the beginning of time. When the paedophilic defendant talked about the highly spiritual nature of his love for boys he meant neither the Holy Ghost nor the evil spirit. It is likely that he meant 'poetic' in the sense of inspirational. It is suggested, however, that he also unconsciously expressed the split between body and psyche which characterized his sexual activities. The outer reality of his body was, in other words, almost totally separated from the inner realities of his fantasies, so that his body didn't know what his psyche was about or *vice versa*. Not that these fantasies were necessarily fully or even partially conscious. They may well not have been. Nor would it follow that even if some degree of consciousness were present they could be articulated. Just as the early child-mother position is characterized by a division between inner and outer reality, merging with a totally good mother and projection of evil elsewhere, so in the paedophilic love situation fusion with a child substitutes that with mother. As the original situation is pre-verbal, words were not easily available to explain the matter to the judge; the word 'spiritual' was not altogether inappropriate and, for lack of a better word, had to do. On this level—before, as it were, the child has truly become a person in his own right—there is certainly nothing final about the distribution of roles. This is borne out by the fact that in some paedophilic events the roles of child and man are reversible, just as Zeus and Cupid can interchange. This, incidentally, also applies to the question of who is the seducer and who the seduced. The law's assumption on this score commends itself for its common sense, but it is not necessarily valid, and the regressed man might just as easily be the victim of the child as the victimizer.

8

Another important aspect of paedophilia, which could evoke unconscious envy in the so-called normal man, is the absence of sexual competition and comparison. Size of penis, potency, expertise in love-making are all irrelevant in relation to the inexperienced child who has no standards to go by. If the child as well as admiring the man's body and performance also displays fear of the unknown this adds to the excitement of the paedophil and corresponds to an age-old sexual fantasy and behaviour pattern on which the human male's 'moral' desire for a pure virgin is also largely based. Certainly, a deeper aspect of this desire exists and belongs to the realm of the archetypes.

The concept of the archetype has been repeatedly mentioned in this chapter and without it any interpretation of the phenomenon of paedophilia would be incomplete. But since our chief concern is reality—both inner and outer reality—it is necessary to return once again to the problem from a new angle. Critical observers might in fact call it the most important and certainly it is not new to anyone. It has to do with the effect of paedophilic actions on the child who experiences them.

A boy of twelve was brought to the therapist by his mother. He had had 'a very unfortunate experience' when a man had approached him in the park and made sexual advances to him. Since then he had apparently developed symptoms which worried both parents and teachers. He had become moody and listless and had failed to keep up his usual standard of school work. In an interview with the boy by an analyst all this was fully confirmed. He said the man had sounded interesting and was very nice at first, but later he had behaved in a peculiar way and had touched his penis. The boy reported he had not really understood what the man wanted of him but he had not liked him any more. This boy's father had left the family many years ago and had figured as an occasional weekend visitor. Under analysis the boy revealed, not surprisingly, a very strong need for a loving father, although his mother, who had many lovers during the boy's childhood, had often warned him of the unreliability and treachery of men. It turned out

9

that the boy had once or twice before the event in the park felt a strong if transient attachment to a father figure. This particular man had seemed so gentle and responsive that the boy had experienced an unusually strong and warm wave of friendship for him. Once the stranger started making overtly sexual advances, however, the boy became panicky and felt let down. 'Like your father, when he abandoned you,' the analyst suggested, to which the boy nodded assent.

This event affected the child considerably because it broke the most potent of archetypal taboos—that of incest—which also implies an abandonment by father in his role of father. Paedophilia certainly contains this very considerable trauma for the child and no doubt in many instances for the man as well. They both have to suffer for their transgression and when the defendant called his love for children 'highly spiritual in nature', something of the numinous experience which accompanies such transgressions was expressed by him. Once again it is only the gods who are free to commit incest, in the same way as it is perhaps only they who can experience man's apotheosis without perishing. For mortal man, parent and child alike, idealization is a threat to what individuality he may have attained, and with the passing of time it will destroy him as a person.

These introductory remarks are concerned almost exclusively with that aspect of paedophilia which finds its expression in the acted-out sexual fantasies of certain men and boys. In other cases, however, as in 'Mary's Story'—the second of the two case histories recounted in some detail below—it is evident that very real love situations can arise in which a deep and lasting psychic awakening can encompass bodily and religious transformations of feeling that clearly go in the direction of individuation. This occurs when there is sufficient ego-strength available to guard against an inundation by impersonal, that is to say archetypal, contents. While the condition of falling in love is characterized by the superimposition of inner images which belong to the so-called lover or to no one in particular—being impersonal and collective—the experience of love has neither need nor room for idealization. It is concerned with the inner and outer reality of the beloved, who really does live on this earth of ours and not in the troubadour's ivory tower of perfection. For incarnation alone can bring forth the truth of love, and the birth of the child heralds the new beginning, the new age, of man and his individual self. What better symbol could there be than that of the young boy or girl in this process of growth?

JOHN'S STORY

The loved-one sees himself
in his lover, as in a glass,
without knowing who it is he sees.[1]

The complexity of paedophilia is illustrated by the life story of John, a fifty-year-old patient. John was the fourth and youngest child of a young mother who was in her twenties at the time of his birth. She called him Désiré when he was in the womb, hoping the name would be sufficiently neutral to express no predilection for one sex or the other. When he was born his two brothers were aged six and two and his sister was four. His father had married comparatively late in life and was twenty-five years older than his wife. He was a rather self-sufficient scientist, a somewhat withdrawn and distant figure who spent much of his time in his college laboratory or in his well-sealed-off study at home. John remembers him as a benign stranger with a slightly mocking air who was easily amused by his wife's and children's frolics. He never took any member of the family very seriously, least of all his pretty wife and his youngest child. John was often told that he was the exact picture of his mother and remembers that he used to call her 'me-me' when he was small. The others teased him and called him 'me-me' too. His sister

[1] Plato, *Phaedrus*. Quoted by Harry Williams in *Poverty, Chastity and Obedience* (Mitchell Beazley), p. 113.

11

once shouted at him: 'She's mummy not me-me,' and hit him. Nobody else ever did that. They all kissed and fondled him and laughed at him. He was also the declared darling of Nanny, who had been his mother's nanny, and had lived with them from the start.

John was a rather delicate child. He was born two months prematurely and only just survived the first week of his existence. His mother was also very ill and was told she must never have another child. ('Thank heaven for that,' the patient commented.) John was frequently ill. He loved being in his mother's bed in her sheltered room, which had an aura of mystery with its perfumes and dimmed lights, its silver brushes and its comb made of gold. She called it her 'Proust room' because she read French novels in translation and felt herself to be a special person, just as John did. She read to him before he went to sleep and he did not listen but looked at her face and the movement of her lips. She was beautiful, he thought. He stared at her eyes and sucked a dirty piece of blanket which he always carried around when he felt sleepy. He had many exciting daydreams in that room. Most of them had no words, only pictures. His mother was in all the pictures and the two were very close. When Nanny came in it was all quite different. She also read to him and then he did listen. He liked to hear the same stories and got to know them by heart. There was much less mystery now even though they were in his mother's room. His sister visited him too and was kinder than usual because he was ill. It was really much better to be ill: he felt safe.

But very unsafe and rather dreadful things also happened to John mostly at night. He would find himself in bleak, lonely landscapes, threatened by bizarre monsters with red eyes like glowing fire. When he tried to run away he found he couldn't move, and when in despair he called to his mother, a witch woman appeared instead. She glared at him pitilessly and gave an evil, hollow laugh as she came nearer and nearer, and still nearer. He wanted to scream with terror but no sound came. He was on the brink of some terrible darkness and knew he would fall into it when he woke up just in time to find himself in his mother's arms. At first he was not sure whether she was the witch, but she talked to him and kissed him. Gradually he awoke fully and realized it had been only a dream and tried his hardest to forget it all. But the awful pictures often came back and he sometimes feared to drop asleep lest he should fall into that frightful dark nothingness.

When he was not ill John slept in the boys' room. His brothers were quite rough and he was easily frightened. They enjoyed his fears and pretended they weren't his brothers but murderers. He made out that they were lying but he really quite believed them. He knew he must not admit it and must behave as though they were joking, but often it didn't feel like a joke.

When he was five he went to school. It was very frightening. He didn't like the smell of the school lavatory and he shat and peed in his pants rather than go to this lavatory which was so different from the one at home. The other children teased him a lot and called him girls' names. He was afraid of them and got tummy-aches in the morning to avoid going to school. The doctor came and let him stay at home. His mother put him into her bed and looked after him. Then he was back in the golden twilight and felt safe.

But again and again he had to return to school and live through agonies of pain, homesickness and loneliness. One day he found a dead cat in the road—killed by a car, he thought —and was filled with terror. He was told that death happened to everyone one day and would even happen to his mother and nanny and himself. He was inconsolable. He couldn't be- lieve that his mother had no power to do away with death, and it astonished him that everyone seemed to take it so calmly and was able to laugh and joke as if all this darkness and death didn't really exist. How could anybody ever forget it if they had to die? His mother had taught him to pray to God, but what was the good if God let him die in the end? At school, too, they talked about God and had morning service, but God seemed to take no notice of his agonizing fears and his tummy-

13

aches grew worse. He was often sick in the morning and refused to eat lest he were being poisoned and would die even sooner.

John felt distraught with doubts about his mother's omnipotent goodness. Surely she was bound to know what inner pains he had to suffer. Yet she appeared to be composed and not all that worried about him. He wondered why she couldn't change things and make it all good for him. Why had he to go to school and be away from her? How could she think of other things and not be as deeply affected by all the misery as he was himself? He began to wonder if she loved him. She seemed miles away from him. Often when he tried to tell her of his fears she did not understand him and his agonies no longer affected her as they used to. She now said such ordinary things, just like the teachers at school who spoke of one's duty to work and to be courageous and obedient. He wouldn't have believed it possible. He felt betrayed and more forlorn than ever before. Her responses were totally inadequate and apart from occasional glimpses of hope that she might yet understand him and be able to help, he felt aggrieved and alone in a dark wilderness of the soul. The fear of being unloved and unlovable produced in him an intolerable sense of guilt and he now seriously waited for death to deliver him from his suffering.

John often tried to re-establish the feeling of oneness with his mother. Without it he felt powerless, while in their togetherness there was absolutely nothing that could not be tackled. Thus, at least, it had always felt until the disastrous awakening to her betrayal. But however hard he tried and prayed for the restoration of their combined power he never seemed to succeed, and the days and weeks passed in depression.

On John's eighth birthday his mother gave a little party to which she invited some of her own friends' children. This arrangement suited John as there was no one he was keen to ask. Among the guests was a boy who had only recently come to live in this country. He had not yet made any friends and his family was glad of the invitation. Three years older

14

than John, he was a beautiful dark-haired, dark-eyed stranger with a mysterious past in foreign lands where he had spoken a different language. His name was Roberto, and John was immediately fascinated by his appearance. He looked very grown-up and behaved in a sophisticated, grown-up way. John was very pleased by the attention Roberto paid to him as host. He was so kind and warm towards him that John was quite amazed and not a little proud. When the party was over John wanted to see Roberto again, and he even took the initiative of finding his telephone number and ringing him up. Roberto seemed eager to come and play and thus the two boys began a rather unequal friendship which was to turn out to be a milestone in John's existence. John, now no longer depressed or lonely, became Roberto's constant companion during one long hot summer holiday. Neither family questioned the validity of this friendship, and no one except the two friends knew of the depth of feeling which they had both begun to experience. They were magnetically drawn towards one another, and John's siblings teased him. 'Where is your twin?' they asked him. 'Are you his lover?' his eldest brother inquired with all the scorn of a teenage prig. John burst into tears and didn't know what to say. He was surprised and a little flattered by the allusion, but also very confused. This brother had always been vaguely kind to him before, and John decided to ask Roberto's advice as he couldn't understand the whole thing himself.

John's parents owned several acres of forest land, which surrounded their home. One could get lost in the thick, neglected pinewood, and the two boys created a dream castle in it. It was all a secret: they were both royal children. On one warm summer day the two friends returned to their castle and began to play. 'Let's get undressed,' Roberto suggested, and John was thrilled by the idea. In a minute they were naked. 'Look at my cock,' said Roberto and showed John his penis which stood up like a candle. The little boy was flabbergasted and stared, full of admiration. 'I can't do that,' he said flatly, but the other laughed in a funny way and said: 'I can make you.' 'Make me what?' 'Make you stiff. Just lie down.' John lay down on the warm earth covered with pine needles. 'Are you sure you want me to?' asked Roberto. 'Of course, go on,' said John. Roberto knelt down by his friend and began to play with his body. He stroked his tummy and groin and ordered him to open his thighs. John was gripped by excitement and only a little frightened. He let Roberto do as he liked and when he raised his head he saw that his cock had in fact become stiff too. 'Feel it,' ordered Roberto. He felt its hardness. 'Now feel me,' was the next order. 'You see mine is harder and bigger,' Roberto explained, 'because I am bigger than you.' So they went on for some time. Then John remembered that there was some question he wanted to ask. But what could it be? 'I wanted to ask you something, but I've forgotten what it was,' he said, and there was a pause. They both looked at one another. Roberto said: 'You're a sweet kid,' whereupon John remembered. 'Is it true that I'm your lover?' he asked. 'Henry said I was, but I think he was teasing.' Roberto was silent. Then he suddenly bent down and kissed the other's cheek. 'Does that mean you love me?' John inquired. There was no reply but Roberto kissed him again. His cock was still stiff and he rubbed it. Suddenly he stopped and got dressed. He gave John a little nudge and they went away without another word.

That afternoon's adventure turned out to be the beginning of an all-important relationship. For six long summer weeks they met almost every day and played with each others' and their own bodies. The princes' game thus became much more exciting and secretive. No one else knew of it, but it was obvious to everyone that John was no longer sad and lonely. While he loved Roberto with all the passion of his eight-year-old body and soul, he was actually a little less keen on the cock-rubbing aspect than was Roberto. They had some rows about this and the older boy called the other a spoil-sport when he wanted to play other games. John was very hurt and threatened to stop the friendship, but this was nonsense and they both knew it. 'What is it all about anyway?' John would

16

occasionally ask, but he neither expected nor received much of an answer.

When September came both boys were sent to different boarding schools. John suffered from intense homesickness but he and Roberto did not resume their former relationship and they met only occasionally during subsequent holidays. They quickly grew away from one another and were shy and distant. But John never forgot that 'most glorious summer' as he called it, and though the outer Roberto ceased to play any part in his life, he seemed to contain an inner Roberto who was all his own. This 'Roberto figure', which he was to carry with him over the years, felt like a living fountain of goodness, as essential to his continued survival as the real outer Roberto had been at the time of his separation from his mother.

Apart from homesickness, John was not altogether unhappy at school. He found work easy and was quite good at games. He was fairly popular with the masters as well as the other boys though they tended to tease him about his prettiness and over-polite behaviour. Quite a bit of cuddling and fondling went on among the boys but John did not join in more than was necessary to avoid being called a prig. He usually remained aloof and very much preoccupied with his own body and his own private thoughts. Roberto's picture became misty but gained rather than lost in its magical quality. Although some of the bigger boys paid him compliments and told him that he was nice-looking, he never really believed them as beauty seemed the prerogative of Roberto's image inside him. He wanted to look like Roberto, but since he was fair this was, he argued to himself, an impossibility. He prayed to become Roberto. He tried to will himself to be like him, but nothing worked and he remained dissatisfied with his own looks which he studied in the mirror whenever he had the chance.

When he reached the age of puberty he kissed his first girl. She was a little older than himself and had dark hair. They were both passionate. He felt she was a bit like his mother, which both frightened and pleased him, and also like Roberto, which was good. It happened during the school holidays and

17

he was at times so overwhelmed by his feelings for her that he couldn't bear it. He wished he had never known her and at the same time dreaded their forthcoming separation as if it were the end of the world. In spite of their passionate kisses they never touched one another's bodies. This was mainly due to his fears and had vaguely to do with his mother and also with the terrible knowledge that he was not Roberto and therefore could not compete. He masturbated more than ever, but it was never for Lucy although he had a terrific erection when they kissed. All his sexual imagery remained glued to Roberto. Other sensual thoughts and feelings were not consciously permitted and he was somehow walled in, divided between inner and outer events. On his return to school he wrote a letter to Lucy and began to masturbate with her in mind, but when the next holidays came he was glad she had moved elsewhere, and her image faded.

He had become quite close to his mother again, but still felt the boundaries between them. He could not talk to her about his sexual feelings because he feared she would probably not understand him. He barely understood them himself, and this made him feel lonely at times. Then again his mother looked rather sweet and loving; surely she knew what was going on in his turbulent soul.

When he was sixteen he was made a prefect at school. He now had responsibilities for others and according to the rules he was expected to cane some of the boys. The other prefects made no secret of the sexual excitement which caning gave them, but John was astonished and even outraged by their frivolous talk and once more remained aloof and withdrawn. However, one day he did decide to cane a rather pretty little boy who had been cheeky and provocative for weeks on end. Having obtained the housemaster's permission, he told the boy to report for a beating after evening prep. All through the afternoon he felt a growing excitement and was far more terrified than his victim when the appointed hour came. His teeth chattered, but he was not conscious of any sexual excitement when he ordered the cheeky boy to bend over and receive his punishment. Suddenly he realized that the boy reminded him of Roberto, and this made him almost choke with emotion. He gave him three ferocious strokes with the cane and had great difficulty in keeping control of himself. He heard himself send the other away as if it were not he who spoke. The boy left the room in tears, and as soon as he had gone John collapsed. He felt a mixture of violent sexual desire, great guilt and passionate love. He cried and masturbated himself to sleep.

For several days John lived in a nightmare. His lust for the boy Philip seemed the only thing that existed. At the same time he was beset by the most terrifying scruples, which were caused by his lust as well as the caning. A week later he invited Philip to his study, had a long talk with him and at the end kissed him. Before the term was over they had become lovers in the pinewoods. John's violence and the intensity of his greed for Philip were enormous. Philip, secretly called Roberto, was sweet and responsive and the fulfilment of their relationship outweighed all scruples. John felt reborn. As the term passed their sexual attachment to one another grew and their masturbatory orgies reached higher levels of excitement. But John did not care all that much for Philip as a person. He found him beautiful and enjoyed their mutual randiness, but once the kissing and masturbating were over and they had both come, he found Philip a bit of a bore. His chatter and cheek easily irritated him and he was not really interested in the younger boy's stories of his family and friends. He did not always listen, just as he had not listened to his mother reading to him when he was a little boy. But while he had been enchanted by her and had, as it were, drunk in her features, Philip left him cold except in their sexual play. This vaguely worried him as it was so totally different from the image of his love-making with Roberto. When the term ended he did not feel at all heartbroken by the temporary separation from Philip, though once he was at home he longed for him and masturbated feverishly with him in mind. As the holidays drew to an end he grew very excited and could hardly wait to see

19

Philip. Their reunion was passionate and for a short time John felt as if he had attained total happiness.

Only a week of the new term had passed, however, when John made a rather disquieting discovery, which was followed by a second even more disturbing one. First, he found Philip making love with another boy. He had gone for a walk in the pinewoods when he suddenly heard excited voices and suggestive noises. He carefully crept in that direction and saw Philip and another chap from his house stark naked masturbating each other. He was outraged and felt cheated and betrayed as he had not done since the great let-down by his mother. He forgot his own former lack of feeling for Philip and felt sick with jealousy and murderously angry. Philip could never have loved him at all if he was capable of such foul deeds. Later he made a violent scene in which he severely scolded Philip and spat acrimonious accusations at him. They made it up, but it was never the same again. The second even worse discovery was that after a day or two John found he did not really care. Within less than a week he himself had become unfaithful and was masturbating with another boy. He found little Gordon utterly enchanting and far more beautiful than Philip. Thus began John's promiscuous career in which he kept faith with no one, so he told himself, except his image of Roberto, which by this time had become completely detached from any real boy who might have once existed.

At university John at first felt as forlorn and insecure as when he was eight and a new boy at school. He joined the athletic club and other societies but remained a loner. The other undergraduates were keen on drinking and talking about 'birds', and he was bored by them. He met a rather beautiful-looking chap who wanted to make love to him, but he wasn't very keen. He didn't much care to kiss and be kissed by a man with a skin prickly from shaving. It was bad enough to have to put up with his own hairy face and body: the loss of his smooth skin and pretty child-features made him sad whenever he thought of it. He sought consolation in physical relations with pretty children. He was attracted by almost any pre-adolescent or adolescent little beauty, and he compulsively cruised the early evening streets in search of them. Roberto was never far away but Lucy, his first girl friend, also made a sudden come-back in his imagery.

This is how it happened. One summer's day he was strolling through a park in the town when he came across a very striking thirteen-year-old nymphet. She goggled at him and smiled. He smiled back and blushed. 'Give me a cigarette, Mister,' she said. Goodness, how exciting! he thought. Cigarettes were erotic things anyway. He didn't really like them, but Gordon had smoked for kicks when they were at school and he remembered how they had walked about in the pinewood naked and smoking. He sat down next to the girl on a bench. 'I'll call you Lucy,' he announced. They stared at each other and as they were quite alone in the twilight he suddenly found his hand between her legs. This had become almost a habit with the boys during his last year at school. He didn't go in for long and complicated rites of seduction but just felt for cocks and balls, and usually the result of such a straightforward approach left nothing to be desired. How odd, the nymphet had no stiffening cock between her legs. Of course, he knew she couldn't have one since she was a girl, but it still came as a surprise. It was very exciting though because she didn't make any protest, and in no time he had slipped his hand underneath her panties and touched her cunt. She remained passive but opened her legs ever so slightly. He began to play around with her, and she giggled. He did not quite know what to do next. After a while he put her hand on his stiff cock. He was emotionally confused by this experience. Outwardly his new Lucy was the child but in an inner sense *he* was the younger of the two, and after all *he*, not she, had the cock. As she seemed vaguely interested John's excitement grew. He was again the boy with his mother and however different it was in every other respect, a merger was forming again, and with it some half-forgotten promise of that particular power which was associated with lovability. This at least was what he felt, though love wasn't really what he was

21

seeking. It was not the girl but her cunt that he lusted after, and more than anything her hand on his trouser-covered cock. If it had been a boy's hand it wouldn't have made much difference, provided it belonged to a pretty child and he could identify it with the Roberto image and himself. Her acceptance of his body, however passive and slight, made this kind of identification possible. John did not experience her as a person in her own right.

In the following weeks they had several meetings. Gradually they became quite fond of one another, though they hardly ever communicated in words. It was all touch and cuddles and occasional kisses. He took her to his room and they undressed. She had no breasts or pubic hair and was therefore not at all frightening. He taught her to masturbate him, and gave her money which she took without saying 'thank you'. He, not she, was really the central figure, though in this kind of fusion it makes little real sense to speak of a centre at all. By paying her he paid for the right to disregard her and live entirely in his own fantasies.

This adventure gave him new ideas or rather added to the existing imagery. He again looked for young boys and now also paid them. It had not occurred to him in the past that he could pay for sexual services, and now he found great excitement in doing so. A fourteen-year-old boy called David was particularly keen and uninhibited, and John felt emboldened to enlarge his sexual programme. He sucked David's cock which he found very exciting. He was reminded of very early events which remained rather shadowy but had to do with the almost forgotten blanket sucking of his early childhood. Thus it also linked up with his mother, though any thought of a more direct contact with his mother's body was absolutely taboo. The idea of her breasts particularly made him flinch and lose all sexual excitement. He even recognized some ill-defined sensation of guilt—but he always put off thinking about it.

Days, weeks and months passed and John continued his masturbatory life with young boys and girls as well as with himself. He discovered little girls' breasts which grew large when

22

he sucked them, not as large as boys' cocks, but arousing in him hardly less excitement. This excitement still had little to do with the whole girl or boy, only with their cunts and cocks, nor with the whole of himself but only with his mouth, and his own cock; it did not envelop the whole of him. Yet he always found new treasures in the objects of his lust. He discovered how exciting buttocks and anuses were. Buttocks were almost like breasts, and if he was lucky in his choice they could be handled much more roughly. One of the boys invited him to smack his naked bottom and eventually they took turns in caning each other. It was all very impersonal and this made it exciting. It felt safe because it was neutral, unlike his early relationship with his mother which had never really been safe. As a very small child he had not known how dangerous she was in spite of the witch dreams, but when she let him down he never got over it. He was determined that such a let-down would never happen to him again.

John heard that some boys and girls went in for fucking and buggery, and this amazed him because it sounded too intimate and personal. He also thought that being inside other people's bodies might be dirty. It was an unattractive and even perilous idea! Again this had something indefinable to do with his mother.

John was for ever thinking about all these matters. However, the reader should not imagine that his whole time was devoted to masturbating and sucking cocks, breasts, cunts and arses, and that he was only concerned with canings and lustful activities. This was not the case. He studied philosophy and comparative religion; he dabbled in psychology and had acquired some basic knowledge of anthropology. In his own way he was certainly a seeker after the truth. Thus, as I mentioned before, he was frequently troubled about the appropriateness or otherwise of guilt feelings in connection with his sexual adventures. Having received a conventional Christian education and being particularly well versed in various systems of ethics—a field which greatly attracted him—he was, of course, aware of the sinfulness of his life. Yet this awareness was mainly intellectual

23

and did not involve his feelings. This at least seemed to be the case whenever he thought about it. On the other hand he had a highly developed aesthetic sense. He was strongly influenced by a study of the classics and magnetically drawn towards literature, music and the arts. The description, by the eighteenth-century German archaeologist Winckelmann, of the Greeks (particularly of Greek youths) touched his feelings more deeply than any moral pronouncement. Winckelmann's words 'noble simplicity, quiet dignity' appeared to him the expression of a deeply religious sentiment which he had no difficulty in applying to his sexual exploits. He saw himself and the boys and girls 'connected' (though in reality unconnected) with him in this light and idealized his fusion with them much as he had idealized the original fusion with his mother. It was fusion—not relationship—that he always experienced. In a relationship there must necessarily be two people involved with each other; in a fusion or merger the two have melted into a single unit and there is no divide across which love, aggression and a variety of contradictory impulses can form a bridge. Neither John nor the objects of his lust ever experienced one another in any separate wholeness. Nor were their feelings whole. The thrust of love-making was divided between masturbating and caning; money payments protected them against involvement, sexual self-centredness against two-ness. Two cocks, or else one cock and one cunt; never two people. No duet to be sung or played. One-ness without wholeness. This was what happened. In spite of all the activity and lust it was almost a non-event. John only perceived this dimly and went on searching and seeking, not knowing what it was he really needed.

John had few friends. His paedophilic life contributed to his isolation because he usually felt rejected when he talked about his obsessional desires. Both homosexual and hetero-sexual friends and acquaintances tended to raise their eyebrows or even refused to listen to his tales. There was a small number of people who shared his sexual tastes, but most of them lacked his poetic and romantic feelings. This was a very

24

subtle point because both his sexual acts and the language which he used might have sounded crude in the extreme, but to him words like 'wanking' had deep beauty and were beloved fetishes. They had sacred meaning in the same way as 'his children' were like sacred beings to him. This holy quality was reflected in the impersonal nature of his sexual ploys which, he felt, were beyond the personal—mysterious and eternal.

In his thirties and forties John's passion for children continued and he found the same measure of limited fulfilment as generation after generation of pre-adolescents and adolescents reached adulthood and ceased to be eligible. The search for new children, new only in detail, similar and wholly familiar in essence, continued unabated. He still lived with the unsolved question of guilt versus innocence and found it impossible to decide the answer. Was he really a seducer of the young, as implied by the law and by many quite sane and unprejudiced people? Or was his a priestly task, reminiscent of ancient customs in pre-Christian times? John wrote poetry which was admired by many. He was also inspired to compose music, and it appears that he was more liked than disliked by those he came in contact with. Strange as it may seem, he appeared to have no enemies among those who had at one time or another been his sexual partners and indeed with some of them he long remained good friends.

When his mother died he mourned her as if his world had come to an end. Of course, it had not really ended but there was a temporary stand-still. He felt as forlorn as when he had first lost her as a child. After a time life went on as before and his sexual needs increased. A new inner element emerged, however, which frightened him. He had dreams and fantasies of suicide and of one of 'his' children dying with him. He saw a possibility of permanence in such an ending; it was as if he might regain his own youth and keep it for eternity through a new and radical union with a beautiful, dying child. As he was to all appearances not a violent person and certainly not what one would expect a madman, criminal, psychopath or irresponsible character to look like, both he and two friends to whom he had confessed these recurring fantasies began to feel increasingly anxious. It was at this juncture that he first sought help from an analyst, who later obtained John's permission to tell his story.

It is not my aim to give a detailed account of John's analysis within the framework of this chapter which seeks a non-technical approach to the problem of paedophilia; but it will be appropriate to make a few comments, based on the analysis. A number of interpretations have already been indicated as the tale was told. The impersonal nature of his love life has been stressed again and again. The early fixation on his mother, to some extent replaced by the fixation on the Roberto image, has been described. And the sequence of events, some inner some outer, speaks for itself. In the first place the lack of an effective father contributed a great deal to John's early confusion and deprivation. To all intents and purposes there was really no father available; no one, that is, with whom John could identify. Furthermore John never felt that his mother was his father's wife, someone to be supported and respected as a person by her husband. His mother was a pretty girl to be made fun of by a man who played the role of a distant father rather than a spouse. John was treated similarly and felt that she was more like another sister than a mother. During his first years he and his mother were not sufficiently detached to be definite, distinct personalities. No real relationship could therefore develop between them at that stage, and instead of relating individually they mainly merged into one. Under these circumstances John never really became a man in his own right. To become a person one has, in the first place, to become certain of one's sexual identity and to know that one's body, penis, soul, intelligence and feeling are really one's own by right. None of this happened to John. He called his mother 'me-me' and tried to make himself into her or make her part of himself. Early events have a greater impact than any later experiences. When John's fusion with his mother proved impossible to maintain,

26

as was bound to happen sooner or later, the highly idealized, omnipotent 'union' collapsed and he became depressed. This would not have been a disaster had they both possessed sufficient identity to replace the former fusion with a real relationship. But there was *not* sufficient identity; not sufficient feeling of being a whole person; on one hand a boy, and a son; on the other hand a woman, and a mother. So John fell into the same kind of idealized confusion with Roberto as he had done with his mother. It was not literally the same, but it was the same in essence. Their homosexual relationship could have been a strength and could have helped them to find their identity. But this was not to be. John was not prepared for the world and still lived in his mother's Proustian dream. So things continued to go wrong with John; he was reaching for the stars.

The alternative to the search for the stars would have been to accept a more pedestrian reality. This would have lacked the glamour of his idealized fantasies about his own or Roberto's beauty and charismatic power. Instead it would have brought some healthy disillusionment and a bearable measure of depression. At least John would not have had to fight *against* depressions which resulted from seeing his mother, and what there was of himself, in a truer light; no longer on a special pedestal or in an ivory tower, but as quite ordinary people. Such disillusionment would have opened the way towards relationships and alleviated much of his loneliness. Cunts, cocks, breasts and arses would no longer have remained isolated parts of scattered bodies but could have belonged to real people and formed a whole in the same way in which a baby may find that the mother's breasts—if she is a 'good enough' mother—belong to a whole person. This whole person consists of much more than just good breasts. The whole person also has a body and a face with a mouth and eyes and the mouth can kiss and say words—both tender as well as hard. The breast is no longer something wholly and utterly good (however much the baby may want it to be so). It is also bad and does not give all that is wanted. So the

27

baby also wants to bite it and hit it and be very angry. In John's case none of this was allowed. He did not find the whole mother; he did not find the breast both to love and to bite, the mixture which ordinary mothers and babies really are. There was no biting or scolding; there were no attacks. Instead there was a cataclysmic breakdown of all the idealizing fantasies between himself and his mother and a flight from disillusionment into a world of increasing illusion.

Consequently John by-passed much conscious guilt. If he had seen his mother as ordinary, her breast as an object of his violent anger (and not just of his love), this would have created healthy guilt feelings which belong to the growth of every individual and to the development of every real relationship. As he had not faced this fundamental guilt experience and was not ready for depression, he was for ever puzzling over the problem of whether or not he should feel guilty about his sexual activities. No wonder he did not know the answer since he had missed out on the original guilt—the guilt which was connected with the discovery (to him forbidden) of his mother's imperfections and his resulting violent reactions. To discover such things at the age of eight is simply too late; so he put his head in the sand and tried to make up for his mother's failings by substituting Roberto as a perfect image.

His violence, however, had no place in this perfect image. It was shelved, and only many years later when he was at school and caned Philip did he allow himself to experience it. Yet it remained split off from the rest of his feelings. When he went in for caning breast-like buttocks and later being caned himself by boys and girls, it remained an act isolated from love-making and the love-making therefore lacked the thrust of passion. Hence the idea of intercourse, with all its natural wildness, remained unappetizing. But his hidden violence at long last made a powerful breakthrough, and then he became conscious of suicidal and, to his consternation, also murderous impulses (for such they were) which led him to analysis.

The agonizing discovery of the dead cat came to assume a new significance for John; for it was then that he had ex-

28

perienced the first shudder of fear at the idea of violent killing and death which neither his mother nor God seemed able to prevent or even to be much concerned about. This lack of concern deeply affected him: when the merger with his mother broke up and violence and therefore also conscious guilt towards her were avoided he equally failed to feel concern for her—for conscious concern can only be engendered when a sufficiently separate person exists to be concerned about. Instead, as a substitute, he experienced anxiety about the unavoidable and ever-growing separation from her. Awareness that the separation was about to become an undeniable fact led him to the utterly terrifying feeling that he must be unlovable. For what other reason could he be abandoned by his mother as well as by God? This idea was intolerable and once more he defended himself by banning it from his mind, withdrawing from it as he had withdrawn from guilt, from love, from concern. Thus he fled into charismatic illusions with his stars and starlets and unconnected bits and pieces of his own and other children's humanity. He was still on the run when he came to analysis but all those inner realities from which he had fled had caught up with him. His mother's death had had a much greater impact on him than he could at first understand. His over-reaction to this event was characteristic of someone suddenly faced with the contents of the psyche which had been avoided for a lifetime. Guilt, concern and violence, not wholly recognized as such but all the more threatening, were on the point of descending on him. But once again he attempted to neutralize it all—this time by the aesthetically flavoured fantasy of a suicide pact. This was a cover-up word for a violent desire to kill. Previously he had killed in a devious way by doing away with whole persons—his own and others—but never by crude and direct murder, however poetically disguised.

This and other important discoveries emerged in John's analysis, not the least of which was the incestuous nature of his bond with both his mother and his young beauties. The greatest, most gratifying discovery, however, was that his true

29

lovability was at long last established; it was an undeniable fact which would no longer need the proof of charismatic and mysterious fusions with others. The road to true relationships lay open.

MARY'S STORY

Mary was an ugly duckling. When she was a child she took Hans Christian Andersen's fairy tale very seriously, in fact it was her one hope and consolation. Perhaps she too would one day turn out to be a swan. She venerated her two older brothers and got on well with her sister. Although Mary was the youngest child she was never pampered by anyone in the family. They were rather undemonstrative northern Catholics with high moral principles and somewhat provincial.

She was the only one of the children who went to university, and her parents were proud of her. They did not expect her to marry but they knew she would do well in her job. She became a school teacher and was respected by her pupils and colleagues. Her life at that time was uneventful. Religion meant a lot to her. She went regularly to confession and was truly sorry for not being a more perfect person. Her imperfections lay mainly in her impatience with her pupils, greed for sweet cakes, and occasional impure thoughts concerning bowel motions and urinating. She took these sins more seriously than the priest to whom she confessed them who often gave her a benevolent smile both before and after the pronouncement of absolution.

At the outbreak of World War II she was almost forty. Someone had once told her that forty was a threshold and that her life might then take a new turn. She wondered if there really were some truth in this as her school was evacuated from an industrial town, to a small Yorkshire village where she had the almost complete care and responsibility of a group of eight fifth-form boys and girls. These pupils boarded with her because the school, through lack of accommodation, had been split into small units under some of the senior staff.

Mary was pleased with this arrangement. Although there was no Catholic church in the village there was a romantic little fifteenth-century chapel in a nearby hamlet. This was turned over to their use and the fat old priest gave them all a hearty welcome.

Mary had known some of the children previously but now she had an opportunity of making their more intimate acquaintance. They were nice kids, she thought, and it was a joy to work with small classes. Instead of just instructing them in English and History, she now had to teach them all the subjects they needed for School Certificate. She had to work quite hard at her own French, Geography, Science and Maths in order to become proficient enough in these subjects, and she also took Physical Training and cross-country walks, which were particularly popular with everyone.

Under the supervision of the old priest she also taught Divinity. This led to an even closer relationship with some of her pupils, as Mary took a very personal interest in their spiritual wellbeing. She had always been a bit of a mystic and took this unexpected opportunity to talk to an appreciative little assembly about the lives of the saints and holy men and women, among whom St John of the Cross and Meister Eckhart had always been her special favourites. The children's religious instruction had until now been of a far more conventional kind and this new aspect of Christian experience was strange and exciting for them.

There was one particularly attractive little girl called Jane among her pupils. Although Mary avoided favouritism (other than for certain Catholic martyrs and saints) this fifteen-year-old girl was an orphan and needed her attention and interest more than the rest. Jane sought Mary's company when they went for walks and began to regard her teacher as a very special person. Jane felt she could talk to Mary, unlike the other adults, without having to pretend that she was a goody-goody. She was able to say all sorts of things which she would never have dreamt of saying to anyone before, and

31

Mary was a good listener and her own child-like heart responded to Jane's.

On Whit Monday Mary and her pupils had planned to go on a long excursion on the moors. There was to be a picnic and they all prepared for it excitedly. However, Jane suddenly felt unwell and was unable to go on the excursion. Mary did not like the thought of leaving her behind on her own and when the priest suggested that his visiting nephew should take the children and Mary should stay behind with Jane, she agreed gratefully.

Jane was especially pleased. Once they were alone she 'picked up' and Mary enjoyed the child's obvious delight. They went to Mary's bed-sitter and Mary made coffee. They chatted and after a while the girl asked if she could lie on the bed. 'I am still a little tired,' she said. She settled down on the bed and shut her eyes. After a while Mary looked up from her book and found Jane staring at her. 'Hullo Jane,' Mary called, 'how are you now?' 'I feel a bit lonely,' came the answer. 'But I am here with you, aren't I, Jane?' 'Come and sit here,' the child whispered. Mary had a peculiar feeling in her stomach and hesitated. 'Do come,' the other insisted. And Mary obeyed.

They sat in silence. Then Jane felt for Mary's hand. She held it and Mary became aware of the girl's fingers pressing quite hard against her palm. 'Are you still unwell?' she inquired without conviction. 'I love you,' the child answered. 'Please kiss me.' Mary felt very awkward but she kissed her all the same. It was a kiss on Jane's cheek. The grip on her hand loosened and the child sat up. She smiled broadly and suddenly threw her arms round Mary's neck. 'Please, please love me,' she said.

Mary blushed crimson. She had no idea what was going on inside her, but it felt like an explosion. She was sure that something was wrong but she had lost her usual certainty. 'What in heaven's name?' she asked in an attempt to sound stern, at which Jane burst into floods of tears, turned away from her and sobbed in a heartbreaking fashion. Mary now took over. She stroked and fondled the girl and tried to calm

32

her down. She wanted to do everything in her power to help, and she produced all the North country common sense she was capable of. 'Look, Jane,' she said, 'I really am very fond of you. Do pull yourself together and tell me what is the matter.' Jane smiled bravely through her tears and said with a sob, 'I don't know.' She shook her head and repeated, 'I really don't know.'

In fact, neither of them knew. But they calmed down and after a while Mary suggested they say a prayer together. Later they went for a walk and Mary took the initiative in holding the child's hand. The hand struck her as very beautiful.

From that day on they became even closer. They both looked for opportunities to be alone together. Neither of them ever referred to the fateful Whit Monday but both were in a new way conscious of the other.

Mary also became conscious of Jane's moodiness. One day she would be gay and full of smiles, and within minutes she could become tense and silent. Mary decided to have it out with her because the girl had begun to oppress her, and she couldn't cope with it. 'Look Jane,' she began, 'what is the matter with you? You are a very moody girl and I don't know what to make of it.' They were alone in a wood and Jane said nothing. Mary was bewildered by the child's stare and felt even less sure of herself as Jane continued to stare as if in a trance. 'Will you sit down on this stone?' Jane said suddenly in a laughing voice. 'Shut your eyes and only open them when I tell you. It's a game.' She was such a playful girl and Mary was always relieved when her gay mood returned. 'Now she is her old self again,' Mary thought. So she shut her eyes. 'You can look now,' the girl shouted a minute later. Mary opened her eyes and before her stood Jane totally naked. She was dumbfounded and felt deeply shocked. 'Get dressed immediately,' she heard the sound of a mechanical voice which did not seem to be hers. But Jane did not move. 'Please look at me,' she said and the words sounded as if she were a small child wanting to show off to a grown-up. But only the words, not the feeling behind the words. These feelings came from a great depth. Mary

33

felt unable to move yet something inside forced her to look at Jane. It was as though a powerful magnet were at work and she went on looking at the child for what seemed an eternity. While looking she also began to see her. Her little breasts stood out like red blossoms and some delicate velvety fluff covered her pubic region. Mary felt overwhelmed, flooded by indefinable feelings, and finally she burst into tears. This frightened Jane and she began to cry too. She wanted to comfort the older woman and flung her arms round her, pressing her naked body against the other. Mary let it happen without protest and they remained for some time in this unequal embrace. Suddenly, Mary felt something like fire inside her as if she had been set aflame and was going to turn into ashes or melt away. She couldn't prevent it and had not even the will to fight it. She gave in, covered Jane's lovely body with passionate kisses and sank into an abyss of infinite bliss.

When she came to, Jane was sitting beside her, fully dressed again, but she knew that it had not been a dream. They were silent. Then Jane said, 'I want to pray and thank God right here and now that we love each other.' But Mary had not thought of God in the very least, and she sat up and felt even more troubled. Surely, she thought, this terrible, beautiful, lovely, quite unforgivable, yet superb event could never have happened if she had thought of God. Or was she wrong? Jane talked as if God had not only allowed it but had positively sent it to them as a gift, a sign of his grace. She was so confused that she could only think of saying a Hail Mary as she always did when she was puzzled or upset. It did help although she had hardly expected it to and she felt more at peace.

But now she needed to be alone and 'think'. It was a long time before she could begin to understand what had really happened between them. A new dimension of experience seemed to have opened up to her. She felt that she had never before really possessed a whole body or a whole soul. A great new task now lay before her. Some vital part of herself had been asleep for four long decades. This child had brought it all to life and she would need her remaining years to bring it to

34

fruition—to a more essential fulfilment. Although Jane was so sure of their love for one another Mary could not—not yet—know whether their love would endure. All she knew was that something momentous had happened to them both. Jane had found someone who loved her body and soul, and Mary had, through the outer child, discovered her own body, which was her own child-self.

They both told this story of their first love many years later. During the intervening years Mary has not become a swan but instead has become herself: a more real human being; a woman in a sense that she had not been before: a lover. Although Mary remained unmarried and never had an outer physical child of her own, her life is creative, and her relationship with Jane remains important to them both and to others who know them. They have both remained faithful Catholics, but what they confessed to the priest and what they withheld, they have never revealed.

2
Paedophilia:
Normal and Abnormal

Rosemary Gordon

I

Paedophilia is a term that has tended to be used only for the love of child or youth in its pathological sense, that is for behaviour or experience where to speak of love is out of place since there is not one whole person relating to another whole person.

And yet the understanding of man gained from biologists, physiologists and the theoretical and clinical work of analysts, suggests that pathological phenomena rest upon normal drives and endowments. These normal drives fulfil necessary functions in the survival and development of the individual and his children. Pathology is merely the unfavourable outcome of the vicissitudes of such drives and endowments.

On the whole the term paedophilia has denoted attraction to and the seduction of a male or female child, though the seduction of the female child has tended to be regarded with more horror and aversion than the seduction of the male child, at least until recently in Europe.

The sexual advances made to children generally take the form of genital exhibition, verbal approaches through the use of exciting or shocking sexualized words, caressing the child's genitals, or persuading the child to manipulate the genitals of the adult. The impulse to seduce children occurs much more frequently in men than in women, and it can take either a heterosexual or a homosexual form. Later I will discuss the possible reasons why, at least up to now, women have been less prone, or have been regarded as less prone, to seduce children.

When we consider the problem of paedophilia we need to search for its normal and healthy roots. They are not difficult to find. Clearly the love of child and youth is primarily a force which protects the young against attacks from adults—both of his own species and even of members of other species; it is also an essential ingredient in that drive that binds parents to their children and evokes their affection and tenderness. The ethologists have done interesting research in this area, showing that the physical characteristics of the young of all species inhibit aggressive-destructive behaviour. Talking of the parental instinct, Konrad Lorenz, for instance, writes: 'It is a distinct and indubitable sensuous pleasure to fondle a nice plump appetising human baby. Furthermore I can assert that my pleasurable sensations in fondling a sweet human child are of the same quality as those I experience in fondling a chow-puppy or a baby-lion.'

The visual characteristics which elicit the parental response seem to be:

(a) a short face in relation to a large forehead
(b) protruding cheeks
(c) maladjusted limb movements.

Apart from a description of the *subjective* response to these attributes, Lorenz also distinguishes and describes the *objective* responses:

A normal man—let alone a woman—will find it exceedingly difficult to leave to its fate even a puppy, after he or she has enjoyed fondling and petting it. A very distinct 'mood', a readiness to take care of the object in a specific manner is brought about with the predictability of an unconditioned response, quite especially a strong inhibition to hurt or kill the 'sweet' baby is activated by the innate mechanism in question.[1]

[1] Fletcher, *Instinct in Man*, p. 161.

37

It can therefore be said that this parental instinct impels the adult to feed the young, to guard them against dangers and predators and also to help them, through play, to develop the skills they need in their adult life.

In the case of man this love of child and youth takes on a further dimension because of his need to preserve his own inner child—that is to say the attributes he has retained from his own early beginnings and which include flexibility, playfulness and the ability to grow and learn as well as such qualities as curiosity, innocence of perception, responsiveness and the willingness to open himself to experiences of wonder and awe. All these attributes are present in large measure in the child. If these attributes are stifled or lost, then a man becomes unable to adjust or readjust to his environment, both natural and social—the latter being more variable in man than in any other species. But more than this, if a man loses the child inside him he loses the roots of those aesthetic and symbolic sensibilities upon which are founded all the most essentially human activities and achievements: that is the creation of art, literature and music, religious experience, the sensing of the unknown, the mysterious and the general search for the good and the beautiful. In other words only while child and youth persist as functional aspects inside him can a person be said to do more than just exist. Only when the child inside him has been successfully protected is a person truly alive.

How then can we understand the pathological form of this quite natural paedophilic drive? And how can we distinguish its pathological form from its natural form?

To start with we need to remain alert to the fact that what is considered pathological paedophilia is to some extent determined by social and cultural mores. For it depends in part on where the line is drawn between childhood and adulthood; what drives and qualities are thought to characterize the child; which of these drives and qualities are regarded as normal; which of them are permitted or even encouraged; which of them are prohibited and tabooed. Most societies foster in their members a certain image of a child and an adult. And most societies provide, through the institution of dramatic and ritualized adolescent initiation ceremonies, a sharp demarcation between childhood and adulthood, thus reinforcing in their members the predominant image of child and adult. This, then, facilitates the self-image and the self-identification of the individual who is in transit between childhood and adulthood.

To give a few examples: in many societies, notably in Europe during the last century, childhood and sexuality have been regarded as mutually exclusive. The child's sexual drives and experiences had been so thoroughly denied that Freud's rediscovery of infantile sexuality caused disbelief and disgust. And yet among people like the Trobriand Islanders, who had been studied by Malinowski, infantile sexuality was known and accepted as natural. There children engaged readily in sexual play with one another, and pre-marital sexual intercourse was tolerated and usual. In India child marriage was customary, although the bride was not usually taken into her husband's household until she had reached puberty with her first menstruation. This tended to be the case if the husband was decidedly older than his bride. If the two were more or less of the same age, the bride might grow up with her husband in his home, and the marriage would be consummated when the two were ready for it. In some cultures, like certain Islamic ones, sexuality is considered normal and acceptable for the boy, however young, but not for the girl or even the woman. It is usually quite clear to the members of such cultures that these expectations apply only to their own members and not to people from different cultures. Some years ago a friend of mine, a young Frenchwoman, arrived for a holiday in North Africa. She had hardly stepped out of her hotel, when she was accosted by a boy of about eight or nine.

'Lady, would you like a gentleman?' his little voice piped up.

'Non, merci,' answered my friend.

'Would you like lady?' he piped up again.

'Non, merci,' she replied patiently.

'Would you like donkey?'

'Non, merci.'

They went on like this a while longer, when finally the boy cried out in despair:

'But what do you want? Would you like me?'

She hugged him, gave him a small coin, giggled to herself and promised to make a note of this encounter in her diary.

In Northern Europe the last decade or two has witnessed a considerable shift in the conception of childhood and adulthood, and certainly in the definition of the age limit between these two. Until quite recently thirteen-, fourteen- or fifteen-year-old girls and boys were regarded as children, and sexual adventures were considered impossibly precocious for them. Intercourse before marriage was limited to a tiny percentage of girls, most of whom protected their virginity as an essential dowry for their wedding. I remember seeing a cartoon in the English *New Statesman* about fifteen years ago. A rough-looking chap, a kind of Teddy-boy, sits across the table from a young woman with a tear-stained face, and says to her: 'It may be my baby, but I'm not going to marry a girl what is not a virgin.' In recent years people in Europe have come to expect sexual maturity to arrive much sooner and that it will naturally lead to complete expression in sexual intercourse. Mothers of young girls have transferred their anxiety about whether their daughter is a virgin, to whether she has been supplied with the pill and can be relied upon to take it conscientiously when sexual exploits have become inevitable.

Indeed, one may wonder to what extent a novel like Nabokov's *Lolita*[2] reflected on the one hand a phenomenon that was already in the making and on the other hand to what extent it helped to speed up the development of such a phenomenon. It certainly drew attention to the fact that the young girl is by no means always passive in her seduction by an older man.

[2] Published in 1955.

40

The question of distinguishing normal from pathological paedophilia inevitably leads to a consideration of perversion or deviation as such, both in terms of its dynamic and historical roots.

I consider it a primary characteristic of deviation that the whole is sacrificed for the sake of a part. This conception of deviation derives from Leopold Stein's seminal discussion of 'good' and 'bad' structure—'structure' being understood as the composite form of any given whole—which he developed in his article 'In Pursuit of First Principles'.[3] He advanced the hypothesis that 'structure' is both restrictive and teleological. It is restrictive because:

> a set of limitations on the free play of dynamic elements is precisely what structure means and that in so far as an instinct or archetype remains or becomes unstructured, its action *ipso facto* becomes a crime (or sin) because it is committed in pursuit of the archetype's own end, and thus threatens the structure of the whole, that is, the organism.

In other words, Stein makes the point that 'bad structure' is one in which the purposes of the whole have been sacrificed to the purposes of one of its parts or elements. And in pursuing this theme he has postulated that there exists what he calls 'primary guilt'. This develops when an individual archetype predominates at the expense of the welfare of the whole.

This conception of deviation is reinforced when considered in terms of inter-personal relationships. Here, too, we are confronted with the substitution and predominance of a part against the whole. Thus there tends to be a limitation or avoidance of a relationship with the other person as a whole person. The totality of the whole person, the totality of his needs and his qualities, is ignored and even denied for the sake of a part such as youth or age, largeness or smallness of penis or breasts, red-hairedness, etc. This characteristic of deviation—the sacrifice of wholeness and totality to a part —often goes with marked obsessive-compulsive characteristics.

[3] *Journal of Analytical Psychology*, 1965.

Hence the pervert is often ruthless, single-minded and driven in his need to satisfy his desire.

Perversions tend to derive from and to express preoccupations and anxieties which characterize the various stages of infancy and childhood. In the case of pathological paedophilia there are many who feel sexually ineffectual and insecure, who fear that their penis is too small or too inefficient, or that it might arouse contempt or ridicule in any potential partner, male or female. And many paedophils, as William Kraemer has well illustrated, are still deeply enmeshed in an infantile relationship with their parents, usually the mother, so that they cannot relate to adults as equals, but feel at ease only with children.

In many deviants, and particularly in paedophils, there is an eternal longing for an idealized childhood and youth which is often thought of as a state of purity and innocence. I consider this to be another important characteristic of the deviant, namely his general resistance to change and growth. Fear of change and growth is often closely interlinked with unconscious dependence, diffidence, self-doubt and anxiety lest new situations or new experiences prove overwhelming and so cause a sense of shaming inadequacy. It is true that perverts are often thought of as fickle and unable to sustain any lasting relationship. But this changeability is deceptive. For it must be remembered that, in their case, relationships are formed not with whole persons, but only with certain emotionally changed parts of persons. And it is these part-persons that remain strangely immobile and unchanged, as if the deviant dare not surrender to any true excitement without the reassuring presence of these familiar objects.

This discussion of perversion or deviation may now help us to define and contrast normal and abnormal paedophilia. In some cases it may limit the concept of pathological paedophilia; in others it may actually extend it as, for instance, in the case of women who have been regarded as less prone than men to enact paedophilic impulses. In fact this seems questionable. I would, for instance, regard it as an expression of abnormal paedophilia if a mother could really respond only to babies or infants up to a certain age. Such women often become indifferent or cold and even reject their children once they have passed the crucial age boundary. They may disguise such emotional 'turning away' by developing the 'pumpkin-eater' syndrome: the compulsive need to have more and more babies, always new, fresh babies. Naturally, they would then argue, the newest is the most helpless and needs all their attention. A different way of satisfying this particular form of paedophilia is to persist in treating the growing child as if no growing were in fact taking place. This is by no means uncommon and it can indeed do a great deal of damage, as can be seen quite clearly in the case of Mrs X which I have described below.

Why, then, have women been thought to be free from abnormal paedophilia, or why is paedophilia more readily acceptable in the case of women? One reason is that the sensuous expression of paedophilia in women is socially approved, whether directed to their own or someone else's baby or child, because it is a vital and necessary function of all maternal caring. Equally, there is no social disapproval of a mother's expression of her narcissism if it actually extends, as it usually does, to encompass the baby; for the baby is then experienced as part of her own 'beautiful' body. In fact such an overflow of narcissism can further enhance the safety of the baby. It may lay the foundations for self-confidence and self-evaluation in later life—so long as the mother has succeeded in retracting her narcissism from her infants at the appropriate moment—thus helping them in their mutual differentiation from one another. A mother who lacks a certain amount of self-love often passes on such deficiency to her child, particularly to a daughter. On the other hand, Lorenz's description of the sensuous pleasure experienced by men as well as women in relation to babies and young creatures points clearly to the normality of such psycho-physical reactions in both sexes.

We might then summarize the problem of paedophilia, both in terms of its normal and its abnormal character, as follows.

43

Paedophilia, the love and sensuous experience of child and youth, is a normal and universal phenomenon. It plays an important part in guaranteeing the protection of the young against dangers. It ensures that they are nourished, cared for, and played with as a part of the teaching of skills which they need to acquire; and that they are given affection and the sense of security which will implant in them sufficient confidence both in their own value and in their capacity to deal with life and its hazards. Paedophilia is most easily recognized when it is directed towards an external object, a baby, a child or a youth. However, it also plays an important part when it is experienced in relation to the internal or internalized child or youth, that is, in relation to 'youthfulness' and all that this implies. Here, too, it can develop into a malignant force if the impulse becomes compulsive and predominant; if nothing but the child is recognized, or if the whole of the person demands to be 'young', much in the way of Oscar Wilde's Dorian Gray.

The exploration of some of the archetypal themes discussed by Jung may prove useful here, for they act as valuable signals and signposts, as for instance the themes of 'the eternal youth', and 'the child'. The eternal youth represents beauty, strength, courage and idealism; it represents the willingness to venture forth and take on apparently impossible risks and impossible adversaries—dragons, giants, sorcerers, witches, etc.—in order to safeguard purity in the face of all temptations. When 'the child' appears as an internal figure in fantasies, dreams or myths, it tends to represent growth, and futurity. Its presence as an internal figure reveals a person's 'growing points' and suggests that he has sufficient sap and vitality available for further evolution of personality, for further creative living and achieving and perhaps even for a new beginning. At the same time its presence points to areas of undifferentiation which I consider to be the potential growing points—which are also areas of innocence, of naivety and of a certain trust in people and in life, and of course they also contain the areas of sexual undifferentiation. Here, then, pre-genital impulses and fantasies

44

are dominant, and erotogenic zones, other than the actual genital ones, seek stimulation. Without the existence of such extra-genital areas, the sexual life of the adult would indeed be dull and stereotyped, devoid of the joys of sexual foreplay, intimacy and tenderness.

In the normal person pre-genital desires and experiences contribute to the completeness and richness of the total sexual experience and so orchestrate the principal theme. True, the official and explicit value judgements in Western society, including the earlier psychoanalytic formulations, have tended to overlook or even deny the presence and normality of such collaboration between genital and pre-genital feelings and activities. The earlier analysts, for instance, made it appear that the normal (the mature) person should have left behind these various developmental stages and their associated erotogenic zones, just as a snake sheds its skin.

The deviant person compulsively places at the very centre of his interests and activities what in the normal person is merely subsidiary in his erotic life. And often this becomes the only possible way he can achieve sexual gratification. Thus the paedophil, instead of relating with the child part of himself to the child part of his partner, can only relate to an actual child or youth and needs the concrete reality of such a partner. Consequently, instead of enriching and enlarging a total sexual experience the paedophilic impulse stultifies and impoverishes it.

So far I have discussed paedophilia in general. There is in fact very little literature on it, and what exists is mainly from the criminological standpoint. As an analyst one only works with very small numbers. Thus the work of the analyst might be compared with the work of the archaeologist or the geologist who makes a bore hole in order to get samples which will help orientate him about the general features he can expect to uncover. However, the paedophilic patients who do come to the analyst are likely to be the more exceptional ones compared with those who find themselves in a court of law. They are likely to be more gifted and above all more highly

45

motivated, even if unconsciously, to grapple with their problem, to work at it, to suffer the anxiety and exposure involved in working at it, and to seek to transform it somehow into something more socially acceptable and, above all, more personally enriching for themselves.

The patients who have come my way were essentially homosexual paedophils. My experience is thus further limited to patients with this particular deviation. However, my work with them has led me to recognize some recurrent situations and themes, and I believe that these might characterize the history and experience of paedophils in general. I shall describe some assumptions and reflections, as they have occurred to me in relation to the data of my own patients in the hope that they may stimulate thought and possible comparison with a wider sample of patients, treated by colleagues or other people in the caring professions.

I have chosen to describe here in some detail the analytic work with those patients only in whom abnormal paedophilia was apparently the major presenting symptom, and where the work we did together had been intensive, reaching deeply rooted levels in their psychic development at a relatively early stage.

The most prominent feature that seemed to characterize the history of my paedophilic patients was the fact that they were the object of unconscious sexual seduction on the part of one or both parents. This was almost explicit in the case of Charles; it was implicit but almost enacted in the case of Ralph. In the case of Mrs X this seductiveness on the part of the mother had assumed possessive, threatening and terrifying qualities, and it had a history that encompassed at least three or possibly four generations.

To be the object of parents' sexual fantasies appears to create an enormous sense of vulnerability, humiliation, and confusion, and engenders conflict around the problem of growing up. For on the one hand 'growing up' is desired, but on the other it is felt that it is either forbidden, or else that it is a hostile deprivation of the parents, or that it is anyway

46

utterly impossible because it is being obstructed and prevented by them.

Several different defensive and/or compensatory ploys may be developed in order to cope with this uncomfortable situation. One of the most general ones is the assumption of a façade—in Jungian language a 'persona'—which is meant to give the impression of toughness, coolness, and impregnable adulthood. All the patients I have described here had sought cover behind such a mask, and in the case of Ralph the slightest slipping of the mask, the slightest show of a chink, created quite overwhelming panic.

The frequently encountered sado-masochistic fantasies and preoccupations of the paedophils could be understood as another defensive manoeuvre, though embedded at a much deeper level in the psyche. They seem to have to serve them as a means of re-living and re-experiencing the relationship with the relevant parent but, by reversing the role, the experience is made more comfortable and reassuring. The existence of such sado-masochism gives a clue as to how threatening the parents' sexualized feelings had been to the infant and the child.

In the case of Charles the paedophilia-making situation, that is the parents' sexual seductiveness (in his case both parents were involved), was further reinforced by the parents' apparent idealization of their own childhood and youth. They unconsciously represented the process of growing up and reaching manhood as marred by disappointment, failure, depression and a general sense of loss of paradise.

What was remarkable about my patients was how they battled to secure for themselves some imaginary place where they might exist and grow and be in control, a place, separate and impregnable. An island in the case of Charles; a house in the middle of a murky marsh in the case of Ralph. The nature of their hide-out, its isolation, impregnability and secretive quality all indicate a powerfully felt need in them to find and to establish their own, real selves; it indicates

47

also how *much* protection they feel they need in order to do this.

The strength of the threat of a parent's unconscious paedophilic impulse towards the child probably lies in the fact that it encourages a child's strongly incestuous sexual desires and fantasies. It could thus be more damaging than sexual assault by a stranger. For if incestuous sexual desires become overwhelming, or if they initiate phoney or premature adult sexual feelings and preoccupations then this can militate against the development of separateness, independence and an experience of the uniqueness of the self. An encounter with the parents' normal paedophilia is essential for achievement of this experience of selfhood, but encounter with abnormal paedophilia can vitiate it totally and could lead to a perpetuation of deviation through successive generations.

II

In order to illustrate some of the points I have made, I want now to describe three patients in whom the theme of paedophilia had been dominant.

I will sketch in detail the actual analysis of one of them in order to convey something of the flavour of the feelings and fantasies in the analyst-patient interaction, for they helped me to increase my insight and understanding of the problem of paedophilia. I will then deal more briefly with the other two cases and give their history and experience in summary form only.

All three patients completed their analysis with me several years ago and I have altered a great many details of their personal history in order to safeguard their anonymity. I trust that I have succeeded. But if one of them should come across this book and should recognize himself I ask him to accept my apology—and my gratitude.

RALPH

Ralph was a very big man with a soft but booming voice. He had a crew-cut and an injured right hand. He limped and had a black eye when I saw him.

He had hardly sat down when he remarked: 'I suppose I should ask you how much you charge.' Then he told me that he had been hurt playing rugger at the weekend. He had been to hospital and they had put a big bandage around his left leg. On the following Monday he had gone to work (he taught French and Geography in a boys' grammar school). Aware of his bandage he suddenly felt 'loathsome'. He got into a panic and just left his school. When he got home he removed the bandage. But he had not been able to go back to work. He told me that he had done this sort of thing before: he became overwhelmed by a sudden attack of panic and depression and just rushed away from work and people. He could not bear anyone to see his weakness or his wounds as they would then be sure to attack him.

Ralph had rung me up one Tuesday asking for an early appointment. I saw him on Thursday, two days after his phone call, and a few days after his accident and the ensuing state of panic.

During the initial interview Ralph was both aggressively demanding and dependent and submissive. 'What shall I do?' 'Shall I go back to work?' After a few moments of silence he answered himself: 'All right, I shall go back tomorrow.' And he did. When he came for his next session he remarked immediately: 'Well, it was not as bad as I had suspected.' And he then told me that he felt afraid of work every Sunday evening, but that it was never actually so bad when he got there.

During his first two sessions the following history emerged. He had already had several periods of psychotherapy with various therapists, but they tended to be broken off after a few months. Either he would escape in the same way in which he

49

had recently left work, or he would manage to arrange his life in such a way that therapy had inevitably to be broken off—for instance, by finding a job in another part of the country or abroad.

Ralph was the illegitimate child of an upper-class woman who had already had four other children by the same man. This man had been a civil servant who had left his wife. He had met Ralph's mother and they had fallen in love, but her parents would not allow her to marry a divorced man. So Ralph's father left the Civil Service and took a job abroad. When the grandfather died Ralph's grandmother gave her daughter permission to marry Ralph's father. In the meantime Ralph's father had found another girl, fallen in love with her and married her. Nevertheless, he and his wife returned to Great Britain and the father resumed his relationship with Ralph's mother. He managed to maintain two separate households and homes, which was not unusual in Edwardian times, though he was clearly much less present in Ralph's home than he was in the home of his wife. Ralph's mother was an intelligent, strong and independent woman, concerned to protect her reputation without losing her lover or her children. In fact she managed to use the children in order to enhance her reputation as a generous, socially conscious citizen. She gave it out that the eldest child was her own by a deceased husband; the next two were the orphaned nephews of her dead husband; and the last two, including Ralph, were passed off as Polish refugee children whom she had adopted. If ever the children themselves asked for information about their father or their origin, their mother became stern and forbidding, and all curiosity and anxiety concerning their parentage had to be locked away again. It was only after his mother's death, when Ralph was twenty-five, that he discovered who his father had been.

Ralph himself had become something of an intelligent rolling stone, working in antique shops, in bookshops, on newspapers or teaching English abroad. Eventually he returned to Great Britain and took a teacher's training course. He then found the job which he had when he started treatment with me. When I asked him what had made him take up teaching, he replied, half coyly, half angrily, 'Can't you guess?' He thus made his first reference, though obliquely, to his paedophilia. He then asked me whether the psychiatrist who had referred him to me had told me much about him, and he expressed regret when I told him that he had not because, as he put it, 'that means that I will have to tell it you myself'.

Ralph had been in the Spanish Civil War and it was there that his hand had been injured. But, as he remarked bitterly, 'I was never in an advance in Spain. I feel I am dogged by failures; it is my fate, and its effects spread to all those with whom I am in contact.'

After his first interview with me I had uneasy feelings about Ralph. When I reflected on this after the session I realized that he provoked in me fantasies of actual physical assault. It seemed to have something to do with the way he used his sheer size and bulk. To myself I called him 'King Kong' or 'Caliban'. This unease left me after the second session when he told me of a dream which made it quite clear that he had put into me one of his images of himself and that I had therefore suffered a psychic infection. The dream, which he had had the night before he telephoned me to ask for an early appointment, was as follows:

I am going along a road with a field on one side. Then I see a big, black, dangerous elephant. I am very afraid of him, but when I pass by near him I think he must be very hungry and I ought to give him something to eat. But I go on to the school where I work. On my way back from school I pick some flowers in a friend's garden. I get back to the elephant and then realize that I have forgotten to get him anything to eat. I wonder if I could give him the flowers, but decide that this would be an insult to both my friend and the elephant. Then I am inside the elephant's enclosure—for now I notice that he is inside an enclosure—and there is his shed and in his shed is his

51

keeper, a reddish-haired man, rather little and insignificant. I pass by. Then suddenly I see the elephant come for me at a gallop. I turn and run. He runs after me and catches up on me. I call out to the keeper to save me. He seems impassive but motions me to look round. I see the elephant who has raised himself on his hind legs in order to try to crush me, but he has just missed me. I wake up in terror.

This was clearly an important first dream through which he introduced some of his internal personages to me. It was clear to me that the elephant, angry because of hunger, represented Ralph's hungry, angry and depressed self. And it was probably this huge, hungry and enraged self that had frightened me at the end of the first session. Ralph expressed contempt towards the elephant's keeper, who at that time probably represented me, his analyst, the person outside and apart from him and rather pitiless. But, as I pointed out to him, the keeper, though small and 'insignificant', was in the dream designated as the one person who could control the elephant if he wanted to. His dream ego, his conscious self, seemed aware of the elephant's needs, yet he could not get himself to take care of his needs, or to do anything effective about them, and so the elephant self got more angry and 'he' himself more frightened and more panicked. It was, in fact, left to the 'insignificant' keeper to show him that he could not escape this dangerous elephant and that it could not serve him to run away. He would have to turn round and face the elephant.

In this second session he also told me that he could not tolerate a silent therapist because he suspected that the silent ones really had nothing to say. He felt himself to be a weak, cowardly character: small, squashy and vulnerable. This discrepancy between his real body size and his image of his body size seemed to be the reason why even later in his analysis there were moments when I again had fantasies of being physically, and as it were accidentally, attacked by him.

Although Ralph had described to me only the external

52

facts of his history, the relationship that had developed between us by the end of the second session left me with the impression that he experienced a great deal of greed and that his relationships were likely to be marked by much sado-masochism. Some of the time he would be surly, demanding, and contemptuous and at other times dependent, submissive and diffident. I wondered what age his love-objects were likely to be.

Ralph was silent during many of the sessions throughout his analysis. He would pretend to be so bored that he would appear to fall asleep. At times he would demand that I ask him questions; that I, as it were, press the secrets out of him. Often the silences were broken by rumbling noises from his stomach, so that after a while we came to understand this tummy-language. Sometimes he felt that the very speaking of certain words was dangerous and sullying. There were times when he wished that I knew his secrets and could speak of them, so that he would be spared contact with the words themselves. At other times he thought that he might be able to talk about it as long as it were in a foreign language. But even when he tried to seek refuge in French, it did not really help.

A month after the beginning of analysis Ralph told me the following dream:

I am in a house in the dark; it is full of wild animals, lions, panthers, tigers, etc. I go from the first floor into the basement. I am very frightened, because I am supposed to sleep with a lion. It is still asleep, but I am terrified that it might wake up. Then I go upstairs; there is some commotion. I hear a bell and expect that wild beasts will assail me; to my relief it is my mother—but she is angry that I won't sleep with the lion. Tiger—who in fact was an elderly unmarried friend of my mother's—is asleep on the first floor and she is in control and quite unworried by the animals. She reminds me of the elephant-keeper.

The metamorphosis of the lion-mother theme into a succession of images was indeed to signpost the analysis.

There were a great many associations to this dream and many memories of his early childhood. He remembers that he used to sleep in his mother's bed even when he was seven or eight, though he cannot remember when this stopped. He thinks that she wanted it and his conscious memory is of his wanting it too. Yet he also remembers that he used to put on all the available clothes before going to bed, because bed was thought of as a sort of polar region. He had been told that when he was about two his father came in one evening and was furious at finding the infant Ralph in his mother's bed and had him 'thrown out'. But he cannot remember a recurrence of that scene and, in fact, feels that his father did not come to visit much after that incident. When he was four he was given a new pair of shoes but was warned to hold on to the banister when going downstairs, as he might otherwise slip. He did go downstairs and did not hold on to the banister and slipped and fell. Because he was covered in blood, he was put to bed and greatly comforted. He then had what he called his first 'attack of madness', which, he said, had recurred all through his life. But he refused to tell me what that attack was like. 'That is what I won't speak about,' he said but he could say this much, that when the madness happened he was alone in bed and on his mother's side of it. Only later in the analysis did I learn that he was tempted to masturbate while entertaining sado-masochistic fantasies. These seemed to be connected, in part at least, with the fact that he had dared to rebel against his mother. The rebellion had ended in failure, probably because his need for her and his dependence on her had sabotaged the rebel inside him, and he was left with the conscious experience of humiliation.

After this dream and its associations came a period in which Ralph had dreams which were good and comforting and which expressed a belief that I had allowed him to put a part of me inside him. With these dreams also came feelings of jealousy of other patients or of a possible husband or children of my own. He was angry that he knew so little about me, yet afraid of what he might discover; that he might find in my life a vast number of potential rivals.

One day he told me that when he was about six or seven he went with his mother to a hotel; they shared the same room, but had separate beds. And there Ralph had 'an accident' which made his mother terribly embarrassed and ashamed of him. He remembered that during the same night as the accident he had a dream: 'There is a yellow-greenish marsh and in the middle of it is a little house. I want very much to go and look inside it.' Speaking of the dream he mused that a house in the middle of a marsh is really very inaccessible. So if one lived in such a house no one could intrude. Here seemed to be the kernel of himself: separate from his mother and heavily guarded against her.

A few days after having told me of this dream—which he had had as a little boy—he brought me another dream, dreamt now:

There is a cricket pitch and there is a swamp. But I make a drainage pit. Then it rains very hard, but the pit seems to hold good and does not overflow. However, there are a couple of policemen and they object to this drainage pit: they say it is dirty and fecal and smells bad.

We talked about this dream and wondered whether he might be ready to give me some access to 'his house'.

He came to the next session and brought me something he had written; it was in a half-open envelope. After he had given me this note, he lay down on the couch for the first time, and said that we must now speak in German because German was for him an amoral, shameless language. But even so he found it almost impossible to discuss the revelations that he had written down and given to me.

The revelations concerned his compulsive masturbation accompanied by masochistic fantasies, which were at times acted out. These involved being beaten on his buttocks and thighs, if possible with a mirror fixed so that he could observe it all.

Before masturbation there was the important period of 'the temptation'. This was a period in which the wish to masturbate was mixed with a sense of guilt, fear, and unpleasant sensations in the pit of his stomach. He favoured locations such as empty houses, or woods and mountains. But before he could give in to 'the temptation', he would consult the 'oracle'; he would spin coins of various denominations. He could allow himself to give in only if the coins added up to some multiple of four. His feelings after masturbation tended to be a mixture of disgust and futility and a terror that he might have been seen or overheard. This terror made him 'really miserable'. He had fantasies of having a partner who would be the aggressor, while he would be the victim, but these had never been acted out.

A few sessions later he returned to the sado-masochistic theme and told me that the victim in such a scene must be truly suitable and worthy. It emerged that by 'suitable' or 'worthy' he meant 'perfect', 'youthful', 'beautiful', 'ideal', and that his model for this fantasy was the sacrifice to Artemis, as it was carried out in Sparta, when the most beautiful and perfect youth was sacrificed to the goddess by being beaten to death.

In the following session he told me of the things he had done in his life of which he felt ashamed: they were all connected either with being a coward or an aggressor. This made him reflect upon his relationships in general. He felt he did not really know anything about other people or have the ability to put himself in their shoes because he could not visualize them as anything but 'animated dolls'. Neither was it easy to know what he himself felt like. For instance, in the morning he looked at himself in the mirror and his day would be made or marred according to the reflection of himself he saw there. Thus if he saw himself looking doleful he would be miserable for the rest of the day. It did not occur to him that he had looked doleful because he had started off the day feeling depressed. Again, he did not make any decision except through the use of some oracular device such as coins or cards. He felt so cut off from his own needs and desires that he had to rely on some external agency to plan for him and settle his problems. During this period he had another dream:

He sits on a jetty and suddenly he is two persons. He sits down but then the other personage attacks him ruthlessly with a sort of iron grid which reminds him of the side of a cot. He is very frightened. And then he is alone again, and for reassurance he touches the wall. He finds that there is a wall-paper which reminds him of the wallpaper around his mother's bed. And he wakes himself up by crying out aloud, 'mama, mama'.

This dream pointed clearly to the split inside Ralph, to the murderous fight that went on between the different personages within him.

This split and the sado-masochistic struggle between the different parts of himself now became a prominent feature in his relationship with me. Thus in the following session after a longish initial silence:

RALPH:

Why don't you ask me questions?

ANALYST:

I think you want me to chase you, to burgle your house, the house to which there is no path.

RALPH:

Of course I do.

ANALYST:

And yet if I were really to break in you might not like it at all.

RALPH:

Of course not, but that is your job. If I go to a doctor he asks me questions, and then tells me what is wrong with me. You don't tell me what is wrong with me.

ANALYST:

You think that I have a lot, that I know a lot, but that I

am mean and don't give anything to you. I keep it all to myself.

RALPH:

Yes, you do; you probably know it all but you want me to say it and then you can ridicule me or criticize me. Anyway, why don't you ask me questions?

ANALYST:

Suppose I asked you questions that you don't want to answer?

RALPH:

Well, I need not answer them.

ANALYST:

Then you would really be in control and in a position of strength.

Thus the situation arose in which we adopted the roles of aggressor and victim though the roles switched so quickly that it was hard to know who was aggressor and who was victim. Indeed, in terms of his internal myth of the sacrifice to Artemis, Ralph was really in a dilemma. If he was not the victim it meant that he was not perfect and he had not been chosen; but the honour of being perfect carried with it the pain of being sacrificed to the great goddess. During this stage in his analysis the role of goddess was, of course, projected upon me. If he was perfect then I would destroy him. If he was not perfect he would be spared but I, the goddess, would lose all interest in him. After a while Ralph admitted that this was indeed the dilemma in which he was always trapped, not only with me but with people in general.

A few sessions later Ralph identified more clearly the two major parts that lived and fought inside him. He identified them as 'the child' and 'the adult' and then remarked: 'I hate the child.' I could not refrain from replying with some feeling: 'My quarrel is with the adult-teacher-judge person.' He vehemently rejected my choice as unacceptable, yet a few minutes later he remarked:

RALPH:

I have never written out the second part of the notes I gave you.

ANALYST:

No, you have not.

RALPH:

You have never asked me for it.

ANALYST:

I didn't think you had been in the mood to give them to me; you have not wanted to give them to me.

RALPH:

You should have asked for it.

ANALYST:

You will give them to me when you want to.

RALPH:

So, you want to know?

As this was the end of the session I suggested he might like to tell me about it next time. But he said if that were planned then he would probably not come. He could only talk about it now. So I offered him another session that evening and, contrary to his usual manner, he accepted with alacrity.

When he returned in the evening he settled himself on the couch—in order not to see me, he explained—and for the first time pulled out his pipe and started to smoke it. He then started to speak in French and German.

He told me that he had always made up fantasies in which he was a Greek or Roman hero carrying a sword. But during the last few years the fantasy had changed. He now imagined that he was his actual age, and that he fell asleep and then awoke as a boy aged between eight and twelve.

Soon after this confession he actually met a foreign boy of thirteen and fell in love with him. The fantasies stopped. He told me that what attracted him about the boy was that he was graceful, witty and self-possessed, just as his ideal young hero is self-possessed, witty, graceful and has tact, courage

59

and intelligence. What attracted him so strongly towards such boys was that they looked at things as if they saw them for the first time. They had not yet been disappointed and they expected each day to be fresh and new.

The boy he was now in love with was, in fact, fatherless. One day a café proprietor thought that he and the boy were father and son and Ralph was greatly pleased. He had twice asked the boy to sleep with him and make love with him, but the boy had refused. Ralph said that he gave the boy everything he could think of but that he also beat him, at times savagely. He wanted the boy to excel at everything. He could not help feeling that he had oppressed and persecuted the boy and suspected that the boy resented him and possibly mocked and ridiculed him.

The character and quality of his relationship with this foreign boy also revealed very clearly the enactment of the Artemis myth. But in the relationship with him Ralph exchanged the role with which he identified in his masturbation and which, he unconsciously felt, had been enforced on him by his mother. Now Ralph himself became the demanding, devouring and persecuting Artemis-mother while the boy represented himself, but endowed with the qualities he despaired of ever possessing. He felt that through the boy he might enjoy these qualities vicariously. He also experienced in relation to the boy what he called his 'generosity complex' and felt sure that he would always want to give him all that he asked for, however unreasonable or difficult that might be. Thus he identified not only with the devouring and persecuting mother, but also with the inexhaustible mother. He told me that he believed that all children think of their parents in that way, and that parents can always give to their child whatever it wants and, if they don't, it is because they choose not to. This assumption had really been quite evident in his expectation of me.

Once he had been able to tell me about beating the foreign boy, he was then able to discuss with me the general topic of beating boys. It had already raised difficulties for him at the school where he taught, because parents had complained about it to his headmaster. He told me that the only boys that he hit hard were those between the ages of eight and thirteen who were strong and unafraid; those who, in his terms, were heroic. The ones who were frightened he did not hit hard and they did not interest him. He didn't think that he really hurt them very much; he hit their bottoms with his hands. In fact they didn't seem very afraid of him and probably treated it as in sport.

He felt that those boys who interested him, and for whom he was so excessively ambitious, and whom he hit hard, really understood what it was all about and shared his private language with him.

At this time Ralph began to talk about his father. He had always brought presents for his children when he had visited them. He had sometimes come quite regularly, but Ralph could not remember whether he had stayed the night, except on the occasion when he had been 'thrown out' of bed. His father had been round and fat. Ralph thought that his father had not liked him and had regarded him as 'soft and squashy like a woman'. In fact, most of the time Ralph himself hated his own body. When he was very young he thought that he had female sex organs and believed that a woman had five different excretory organs—mouth, breasts, vagina, urethra and anus—and somehow there seemed to be a sixth, a very mysterious one. He also remembered that he felt vulnerable and thoroughly inadequate when he compared himself with his father. His father appeared to have all the good qualities and seemed able to love everybody except Ralph. Thus from an early age Ralph seemed to have identified his own body with that of the mother whom he both feared and despised. But he projected these reactions and fantasies on to his father, even though at that time he did not consciously know that this man actually was his father.

A few weeks after Ralph had started to speak about his father, he told me that something had happened the weekend before the session. He admitted that it could have been the

61

result of analysis. He had made love with a man of his own age, a friend of long standing whom he had confided in. The friend had invited him round and then set the scene and initiated their love-making.

'Admittedly we each had to imagine that the other was someone else. I had to imagine that my friend was a young boy, but he knows my tastes. My friend took the role of aggressor, allowing me to be in the position of the hurt one, the "victim".' He seemed inordinately pleased about this and found that his impulses towards boys had actually diminished since then. Within a few days of this event he dreamt of a boy aged between seventeen and nineteen who wrote plays. As he himself had sometimes tried to write plays it was clear that this dream figure represented an aspect of himself, but now a little older than usual. And a few days later he had a strangely beautiful phoenix dream:

I see a swan. It is more or less submerged, only its head is showing above the water. I think it is ill or caught up in something and I try to pull it free, but the bird remains submerged. I pull again, still the bird fails to surface; in fact it now submerges totally and I think the bird has had it. But then suddenly it comes up and flies off to the bank. It is a swan, but then, for a moment, it looks like a peacock. Then it is not a peacock at all, but a strange bird. Perhaps it is a phoenix: it has black eyes and a black garish plumage, though not quite as good as a peacock's. But then I think —well, anyone may have a peacock, but no one but me has this bird. Soon I realize that the bird needs to recover and it comes and rests on my breast.

An exciting, beautiful, and encouraging dream. But a phoenix is not a phoenix until it has first died, or in the language of Ralph's dream, drowned. Therefore I should not have been surprised that the next few weeks were marked by Ralph's preoccupation with death and dying, and by a general anger and despair about it. He became silent, withdrawn and resentful again. In one session he complained that he wasn't getting what he really needed from me; that he didn't get enough of me and that whatever he did get from me didn't last. He said: 'One eats, digests and ejects. People leave, and one day one is going to die. Well, better later than sooner. Anyway I feel half dead as it is. I don't write or listen to music or read books or go out.' He became increasingly hopeless and despairing. A week later after a heavy, leaden silence, he said: 'I won't be able to get any better, and I can't be cured for good. No one can be cured for good, because one can't be cured of the ultimate disease—death.'

He stormed out of that session and stayed away from analysis for two weeks. Finally, he rang up and said: 'Oh, I don't think I will come. It is too far. I can't be bothered. I won't be able to say or feel anything.' But he came, thirty minutes late, looked at me challengingly and said: 'Well, I have only come to spite my mother's ghost.'

He then admitted that he felt possessed by her; that she was strong and powerful and that neither he nor I had a hope against her. He had had a dream in which he felt that he was made of 'heavy earth'. In it there was a waterway, but it was dammed up by a sphinx who sat across it, and so the water was stagnant. He felt tired. All he wanted to do was to sleep. He did indeed seem possessed by his mother. Certainly the sphinx was a most appropriate symbol for his mother, who had so fiercely guarded from him the secret of his origins and his paternity. This must have further reinforced his fantasy that her power was indeed mysterious and absolute. Then he told me that just before she became seriously ill and died he had had a terrible row with her and called her 'a liar'. He was sure that he had really killed her and that she died as a result of that row. This made him feel exceedingly uncomfortable and guilty, and yet there was an edge to it: perhaps he was stronger than his mother after all.

Towards the end of his analysis he had another lion dream:

I am in a dry country. There is a lion. I try to escape from it by clinging onto a viaduct but to my horror the lion is up there too. The lion chases me. So I get underneath the arches, only to find the lion standing in front of me there also. But this seems to be a different sort of lion: he is younger and much less menacing. Then there is a woman who tells me just to pass by the lion and that it won't hurt me. And then I carry a kitten and I stroke its head.

Thus the cat family finally became much less threatening and more manageable, and a woman in a helpful role began to emerge and to figure in his dreams.

During much of the first part of the analysis Ralph had expressed great anger, suspicion and dislike of me. He had described me as 'cold' and 'judging', ascribing to me the sort of judgements 'one would expect from clergymen, judges and psychiatrists'. At one point he saw me as: 'A fish hiding under a stone with a long tongue which you shoot out in order to catch on it your victims.' A truly symbolic image of the phallic mother; secretive, dangerous and devouring.

Later his resentment shifted and he then complained that I was not sufficiently active and provocative; that I did not fight and argue with him or chase him with questions. Then he began to suspect that I saw him as 'mushy, soft and pink, like mother'; 'mushiness' and 'pinkness' were qualities he particularly disliked, because if they were characteristic of him, they revealed to all and sundry his identification with his mother.

Ralph left analysis after finding himself a good job abroad. His last dream before he left me suggested that he had after all been able to receive and to take in something from me, something that was solid and valuable. He dreamt:

I am in Africa among a poor and simple people who do not know that they possess great riches in the form of precious stones. These stones are pink or mauve and are probably amethysts. They remind me of stones I have seen in museums abroad; but then I suddenly remember that you have an amethyst in the waiting room.

At that point in the telling of the dream he rushed out of the consulting room into the waiting room to look at it and he returned, delighted. In the same night he had also dreamt of the foreign boy he had loved. In this dream he was concerned about the boy coming to visit him and that he must get him a comfortable bed all to himself.

To summarize: Ralph, the youngest son of an intelligent, upper middle class, unmarried woman, shared his mother's bed until a comparatively late age. He seems to have experienced his mother with a mixture of terror and dependence, and as a woman who demanded that he be for her both a baby and a man. In his sexual behaviour and fantasies he recapitulated the sacrifice of a perfect, beautiful and courageous youth to the Greek mother-goddess, Artemis; a theme which incorporated sado-masochism in his paedophilia. Analysis consisted in uncovering and working through these themes in and through our relationship in the transference.

CHARLES

Charles had been referred to me because of his uncontrollable attraction to pre-adolescent boys. He was a student at one of England's older universities, studying for a degree in English. However, the authorities had encouraged him to leave university for one year in order to have some intensive psychotherapy. So he had returned to live with his parents during that year. They lived in a provincial town where his father had an antique business. His parents, in particular his father, were very doubtful about psychotherapy. They tended to oscillate between feeling that there was really nothing much wrong with him and that psychotherapy was therefore a quite unnecessary enterprise and expense, and thinking that he was really incurable and thus psychotherapy was doomed to failure.

Charles was a lanky youth, with short fair hair, thick glasses, grey flannel trousers and tweed jacket, a typical public school 'type'. In some respects he looked two or three years younger than his age. He tried to appear nonchalant and at ease, but it was quite obvious that anxiety was not far below the surface. He came with a mixture of despair and hope, though he did not really know what he hoped for, since he had no real wish to be deprived of his homosexual-paedophilic attractions and excitements. He told me: 'All I really want is sex. The only thing that bothers me about sex with boys is the fear that I might find myself in jail.' But then he did admit that he hoped that therapy would give him relief from his feelings of anxiety and from a vague but nevertheless real sense of guilt and a tendency to obsessional thoughts which beset him, especially when he tried to study. But he doubted that anybody could or would really wish to help him, a doubt which, I discovered later, characterized his father's general attitude to his son.

Charles was an only child. Both his parents were intelligent and well educated. His father had graduated from the same university at which Charles was now studying. His mother had a degree in languages. As part of her studies she had spent a year abroad. There she had fallen in love with a young man who was an active member of a neo-Fascist party. However, soon after her return to England the young man was killed in a car crash. His mother never got over his death. Instead she idealized him and made him a cult-hero. His photograph was always prominently displayed in her room and he was a permanent presence in the home. Throughout Charles' childhood his mother talked to him about this boyfriend, always romantically. She had married his father on the rebound in an attempt to find consolation, security and protection from the stark experience of this loss.

Charles' father seems to have been the very antithesis of his wife's romantic hero-lover. He had become a quiet, withdrawn man, liable to feel depressed and ineffectual. After what he remembered as a successful and happy time as a student, he had embarked on a university career, and became a very active member of the Liberal Party. But after a few years he gave up his career, bought an antique business and settled down. By the time Charles came to me his father, though still a Liberal, had ceased to take an interest in anything but antiques.

His parents had separate bedrooms and Charles had little reason to believe that there was any sexual relationship between them. His mother had said as much when making disparaging remarks to him about his father's sexual performance.

Charles worked with me in intensive psychotherapy for one year. He was then able to return to college and complete his final year. During that time I saw him only once a week. However, the therapeutic process had by then gained sufficient momentum to be continued even at this reduced rate.

In the course of his treatment Charles stepped out of his public school 'façade' much as a butterfly steps out of its chrysalis. He grew his hair, acquired contact lenses, dressed in increasingly colourful attire and for a while he became an idiosyncratic, exhibitionist dandy. At times during the first part of his final year at college he would arrive for some of his sessions almost unrecognizable in some new outfit. His own affiliations with the British Fascist Party lapsed for a while and then he broke them in a clear and deliberate manner, resigning officially. This occurred after he had recognized, as he himself put it, that the Fascist Party had been a way of institutionalizing his own sadism and that this sadism was, in fact, an over-compensation for his real diffidence and physical cowardice, though it had also enabled him to experience a sort of fusion with other people. His attraction to young boys waned and was for a time replaced by his desire to be attractive and irresistible to older students and grown men. This was the time when he wanted to be outrageous, a real rake, and he did all he could to encourage this impression by drinking and getting drunk late at night while at the same time working secretly during the day.

What had happened to Charles during his treatment? One of the first things he told me was that he wanted at all costs to avoid becoming a 'miserable, depressed Liberal like my father.' He believed that his father was a failure and he also felt himself to be a failure. Charles felt close to his mother who evidently felt an undisguised contempt for his father. He admired her and was in no doubt that she needed him to be a younger version of her hero-lover. One day, for instance, he told his mother about a dream in which he had found himself in the country of her dead boyfriend. 'I am in a house. Outside there is a rebellion. But I have a machine-gun and fire freely into the crowd.' He remembered that after he had told his mother this dream she was more than usually affectionate towards him. In other words it seemed to him that she actively encouraged her son's identification with her lover.

However, later in the analysis feelings of hostility towards his mother began to appear. He then started to remember many long and enjoyable walks in the country with his father, that they used to share an interest in architecture and antiques, and that when he was a child it was his father who used to read him bedtime stories. He remembered that when he was about ten or eleven his father read to him from D. H. Lawrence's *Lady Chatterley's Lover*. But this memory released his suspicion that he was the object of unconscious seduction not only by his mother but also by his father.

It is therefore not surprising—and in fact I regarded it as a token of Charles' potential health—that such double-pronged seduction and encouragement of precocious and freefloating sexuality on the part of both his parents should have incited Charles to seek his own area of retreat. His first token of trust in me, after about three months, was when he let me into the secret of where he really existed: on an imaginary island, which was divided into a number of provinces, all named by him and governed in a way that he had very carefully worked out. A week later he brought me 'the map' of his island and for the next few weeks he shared his island with me, telling me of the various events, geographical and political, as they happened there.

After a time the importance of the island gave way to an increased interest in the actual world around him. Until then I had thought of Charles as a frightened, isolated and touchingly vulnerable person who tried hard to pass for a tough, cool adult. One day he told me that soon after he had gone to university, he had bumped into a 'friend' who belonged to a smart set in college, and how pleased he had been because his father was just then visiting him, and so because of this coincidence, he managed to hide from his father how lonely he really was and how difficult he had found it to make any friends at all.

Charles was overtly and explicitly preoccupied with death, though he experienced it in a highly poetic and romantic form. Having to substitute and to identify with his mother's dead lover was almost certainly one of the reasons for this. Thus he spoke ecstatically of his love of autumn, when all vegetation dies and rots; and of the evenings being the best part of the day, when the sun dipped down in the sky and the furniture of the world lost its colour and sharpness of outline; and of his love of ruins, which spoke to him of time and people long lost in a distant past—the ruins celebrating the crumbling away of what has been. Even as a child he had often indulged in 'delightful' fantasies about drowning. An aunt of his had remarked that the reality was most unlikely to be half as pleasant as his dreams, but nevertheless he could not stop believing that such fusion with the water would be 'rather divine'.

His Fascist political tendencies were clearly, on the one hand, a rebellion against his Liberal father. He felt that Liberalism was the root cause of his father's anxieties and depression. On the other hand, there was his identification with his mother's lover. This link, though obvious, had in fact remained quite unconscious and he did not become aware of it or assimilate it until almost the end of his first year in analysis.

Towards the end of this first year it became clear that his feelings about death, fusion and non-existence were more ambivalent and complex than he had thought when he first came to me. The complexity of these feelings emerged when he began to tell me about his fear of seeing his own face in a mirror. This was based, apparently, on a childhood terror. For a long time as a child, whenever he looked into a mirror he saw himself reflected there with wide-open, staring eyes and dishevelled hair. After a while he recalled that in his grandfather's house there was a long mirror on a wall at the top of a staircase and this mirror reflected the stuffed head of a deer, which hung on the wall opposite. When walking upstairs towards the mirror, the image of his own head and the head of the deer became superimposed, and it looked as if his own head had sprouted horns. As he told me this he remembered a nightmare he had had. He saw his reflection in the river Thames and felt terrified that he would be sucked into it rather like Narcissus who fell in love with his own image in the water and, in trying to embrace it, drowned. In this nightmare Charles experienced drowning not as 'rather divine' but as terror—terror of being sucked into his own disembodied reflection. Moreover, the image of himself as evil frightened and horrified him.

Charles had been brought up by a number of different nannies. His parents took little interest in him until he became a young adult, able to share their intellectual and artistic interests. Little wonder then that there was a great discrepancy between his intellectual and his emotional development. This was further emphasized by the fact that he was indeed very intelligent and gifted. His parents had communicated to him the illusion that their youth had been a period of bliss and excitement; a lost paradise of which they might only catch a glimpse if he, Charles, were to offer them his body and his youth. His childhood and youth were thus represented as highly idealized states of existence, though body experiences belonging to babyhood seemed to have met with little acceptance or confirmation.

After about seven months of analysis Charles began to admit that he found it difficult to get along with his contemporaries and it became clear that he felt at ease only with young boys. This, of course, increased their attraction and made involvement with them so much more reassuring and agreeable. His own penis was so obviously bigger than theirs. He could impress them. He could reverse the role which he had experienced at the age of eleven when his father, talking to him about sex, had remarked drily: 'But actually, Charles, you cannot do anything about it, yet.' Moreover, with young boys there was no problem of orgasm, which for him had become a question of one-upmanship, rather than a pleasure. He tended to think of orgasms as a competition to see who had the better, the quicker or the stronger one. No such questions arose when he was with younger partners. In his sexual approaches to pre-adolescent boys he liked to persuade them to expose their penis while he exposed his. He liked to fondle their penis and often tried to provoke some excitement and pleasure and, if possible, an erection. Then he would masturbate while they watched, and he felt happy if an orgasm occurred, observed by them.

All through the middle period of his analysis he talked a great deal about sex and his sexual exploits. It soon became apparent that most of them happened either in the past, or else only in fantasy. In reality he had no sexual outlets, except for masturbation, which tended to be accompanied by sado-masochistic fantasies, involving beating. Even in these fantasies he was neither the beater nor the beaten. 'It is just a thought,' he told me. 'I am an observer. If I were beating or being beaten in my imagination then I would feel a terrible coward if I did not actually carry it out with someone in reality.' He told me that he fantasized about a boy's bottom being beaten but that it was not a bare bottom, it was covered by trousers because 'if it were bare it would really be too sexy'.

I had often had the suspicion that Charles was not really experiencing his own sexuality at all, but remained an observer, and occasionally a participant, in his parents' fantasized sex life. He had still to discover his own body and his own sensations. He had a whole set of disguises and masquerades to work through before he could dare to *show* himself as he really was. He had to discover himself.

The presence of his secret island had, however, convinced me early on that despite appearances, and despite all the obstacles, Charles was bent on finding his true self. It was because of this that he had constructed a refuge where he, as

71

a person, could become himself. That he dared tell me about this island after only three months showed that his trust in 'grown-ups' had not been completely shattered. The reason for this lay in part in his relationship with his godmother, who also lived with his parents. She was a very important person to Charles. She was quiet, strong and stable and he could turn to her when the world became too confusing. His relationship with her was solid but unexciting. Much of the time I felt that he thought of me in just that way, though it was only later in the analysis that he in fact told me of his godmother's existence and of her close presence in his life.

Charles possessed in strong measure the qualities which Phyllis Greenacre, an American psychoanalyst, has designated as characteristic of the gifted child: heightened sensuality; heightened capacity to distinguish between external and internal stimuli; and sufficient imaginative capacity and arrogance to protect this imaginative world against the pressures of the pragmatic, logical, adult world. This enabled him to retain his potential integrity of self.

Through his paedophilia Charles was identified with both his parents in their idealization of youth. At the same time, by identifying with them, and by becoming like them in their youth, he actually tried to escape from the awareness that *he* was the object of *their* paedophilic desires. The public school façade seemed to be a way of keeping an apparent 'cool' between himself and the world, which initially included myself. For Charles 'grown-upness' meant a general physical and emotional aloofness and asexuality. Thus the idealization of death and decay, in part a sympton of his participation in his mother's fantasies and his identification with her dead lover, was above all an expression of his belief that to grow out of childhood was equivalent to treading the path to the sad and cynical world of his parents.

MRS X

Mrs X was sent to me for analysis by a very experienced and

72

perceptive case worker at the Child Guidance Clinic where Mrs X's daughter, Barbara, was being treated. Barbara was a fifteen-year-old girl who had gradually reverted to a state of near babyhood. She had become excessively dependent, particularly upon her mother, to the point where she was no longer able to go to the lavatory alone. Her mother had to go with her and handle her and clean her exactly as if she were a baby. She had also developed a great number of phobias which further restricted her life. Thus she could not sit next to any man in public—on a bus, a train, or in a concert hall or a cinema. She could not bear to be left alone with a dog, even her own dog. Leaving home and going to school became increasingly threatening and frightening and she was frequently absent. Yet her work had been good; she was intelligent and potentially a quite gifted artist.

Barbara and her mother had attended the Clinic for several months but there had been no improvement; on the contrary her flight from growth and development seemed almost to accelerate. The case worker, who had met Mrs X on a fairly regular basis, began to feel that the root of Barbara's illness might lie with her mother and that possibly more intensive care and concern for her might bring relief to them both. This feeling was based on something stronger than the modish assumption that all mental disturbance is inevitably 'mother's fault'.

Yet when Mrs X came to me for her first interview she immediately expressed very great reluctance to have analysis. She felt convinced that being sent to me was an unjust punishment, and that she was faultless in relation to Barbara and her illness. Although her experience of the analysis as punishment became gradually modified and less painful, it took a very long time before she could conceive that as her analyst I could have any aim or interest other than to help Barbara. That she might elicit my concern and compassion in her own right, quite apart from what happened to her daughter, remained incomprehensible to her for a very long time. Yet here lay the crux of the problem and when this particular trust in herself and in me began to develop, it showed itself to be a real watershed.

It may appear surprising to the reader that I should be calling her 'Mrs X' rather than by her Christian name, as I have done with the other two patients I have described here. Yet to use a Christian name for the person who had come to see me so unwillingly seemed somehow inappropriate. She was a big, heavily built, matronly woman, older than the average mother of a teenager. She dressed in a conventional suburban style: solid shoes, tweeds and a sensible hat. She never failed to wear a hat. She had all the appearance of a powerful and competent woman with determined views.

Mrs X had married relatively late in life and immediately wanted to have children. But she did not conceive for many years and became anxious and depressed about it. When at last she was pregnant the war had started and her daughter was born soon after the fall of France. The political situation and the threat of a possible invasion of England by Germany worried her enormously so that she could not enjoy the first few months with her baby as freely and happily as she had wanted to.

Mrs X lived near London in a semi-detached house with her husband, her only child, Barbara, and a friend, with whom she had shared a house before her marriage. She had trained as a teacher and as soon as Barbara was old enough she went back to her professional work. She had never liked housework and relied on her friend for a good deal of help with it. She loved teaching. She liked getting out of the house, having a profession of her own and earning her own living. She had also had a secretarial training and at some time she taught shorthand and typing at evening classes.

Both her parents were dead. Her father had died in a diabetic coma when she was seventeen. Her mother had died many years later. She had had three sisters, one of them an epileptic, who had died while still a child. There were also two brothers, one of whom had died, also of diabetes, in his late teens. The relationship between the surviving two

74

sisters and Mrs X seems to have been stormy, a mixture of possessive loving feelings and considerable anger, envy and rivalry.

Only a small part of this information emerged in the first session in which she protested about being in analysis. She did in fact keep her next appointment and almost at the very beginning of this second meeting the dam burst and she revealed herself: 'I wish Barbara had a physical illness; then she would stay at home, in bed, and I could nurse her.' She said this so easily, so naturally, apparently quite unaware of how monstrous such a wish might seem to me, a relative stranger. She continued: 'I can't bear that daily parting. I would rather have her go to a boarding school. I wonder what her mock "O" levels will yield next week. Perhaps she won't pass them. I don't really like change. In my experience, change is always for the worse ... Anyway, Barbara does not want to leave me either. And she often cries in the morning and puts her arms around me and says that she never wants to leave me, never wants to be separated from me. She won't even go for a walk with her father unless I come along too.'

She fell silent for a while and then began to talk about the children she taught: how she loved them so strongly that she sometimes resented it when their parents came to collect them from school. How much she suffered each year when they moved on to a new class teacher, though she felt consoled at the beginning of the new term when a new batch of children came to her class. She believed that the children really loved her just as much as she loved them and that they looked on her more as a mother than a teacher. She sometimes went out of her way to give special help to one or other of them. She did a lot of good deeds but somehow they always ended badly. She was never rewarded with gratitude; instead there was usually an abrupt ending and then considerable hostility and undeserved accusations. Her own feeling was that she had an 'excess of maternal instinct. My sisters have described me as "domineering", but perhaps they are just envious. Because neither of them has had any children ... Of course, I was the eldest and as mother was more or less an invalid I had to stand in for her quite a lot and had to "mother" them.' She ended this second session by musing dreamily that if only she could believe in witches and if she were a witch she would make Barbara into a really small child again and then everybody would once more be happy.

This second session left me in no doubt that Mrs X suffered from excessive paedophilia which monopolized all her feelings and attention and which, in consequence, was a malignant force.

The roots of this abnormal paedophilia were laid bare fairly early in the analysis when she told me the following dream. It was a recurrent dream, though on this occasion it contained a whole set of new elements. In the recurrent dream she used to find herself walking over fields and down a long country lane which led to the farm where her grandmother had lived and where her mother had been born. In the dream she visited her grandmother and then walked back. Little else had happened so far. But the dream she now had was very much fuller and richer in detail:

I find myself setting off again to my grandmother's farm, but the lane narrows and there are high walls on either side of it. Barbara is with me, but she is very frightened. I keep telling her that everything will be all right in the end. Then the walls curve over and make a ceiling, so that the lane turns really into a tunnel. It gets blacker and blacker. But I still keep reassuring Barbara. I myself am not really frightened. Suddenly, a man in soldier's uniform jumps out of the dark at us. He seems up to no good. And a whole host of greenflies settle on the three of us. Then the man places something on my mouth; he says it won't hurt, but it does and actually draws blood. It seems that he does this to protect himself against the greenflies. I am still not really frightened, but Barbara is. At times I can see a light

76

in the distance; that must be where the tunnel ends, which is probably my grandmother's house.

In the course of the analysis we often returned to this dream which was indeed a rich symbolic statement about her personal history and how she had experienced it. There seemed to have been in the family at least three generations of possessive and devouring mothers who held on tightly to their daughters. They, in their turn, re-enacted the same drama but with their own role now changed to that of mother instead of daughter. The tunnel in the dream thus represented, in the first instance, the analysis itself, but on a deeper level it symbolized her experience of a sort of umbilical cord stretching from her and Barbara right back to her own grandmother, though this was the end only as far as her conscious knowledge of her family history went. Her great resistance to analysis was therefore not only her fear of the pain she would suffer when her existing way of handling needs and conflicts was examined and possibly disturbed. Her terror was also triggered off by the inevitable identification of our relationship with this possessive matriarchal stranglehold; this was the only form of 'relationship' that she could conceive, for she had known no other.

The sadistic male figure also had both historical and symbolic origins. In her own family the men had been either passive and ineffectual nonentities or they had been unbelievably brutal and savage. Her own husband, on the face of it, belonged to the mild, gentle and inoffensive kind, and indeed she had at first become attached to him out of a sense of pity as he was shy and diffident. In the course of the analysis of her dreams and fantasies I was impressed, as I had been in the case of the other two patients, by the importance and intensity of the sado-masochistic themes. At first the cruel and destructive urges were attributed to the men, though from the beginning she related to such men with considerable affection and in fact was attracted to them. Later she felt herself invaded by hostile and destructive wishes which

77

then were no longer concealed by apparently maternal concerns. The strength and pervasiveness of sado-masochism in paedophils has made me wonder whether such sado-masochism might not be the despairing reaction of the vulnerable infant faced with overwhelming, sexualized, although unconscious, desires on the part of the parents, on whom at the same time he depends completely both physically and psychologically. Moreover, the parents' sexual wishes stir up the infant's own incestuous desires, which he might experience as exceedingly dangerous and threatening.

Only after several months of analysis did the image of the saintly mother collapse. Instead there emerged the memories of an evil, possessive, witch-like person, who used to rush off like a vulture to any newly dead person in order to help 'lay them out'; a woman who imputed black magic to some of her friends and acquaintances; who dabbled in spiritualism and seduced into it—away from Mrs X—the patient's first boyfriend whom she had dared to bring home to introduce to her mother. It was indeed an eerie story that we pieced together in those months. But Barbara got better. Her phobias lessened, her crying became more sporadic and she gained confidence and independence. Mother and daughter defused, so that each could become more complete in herself. For Mrs X this meant that she was put in touch with her own helpless and terrified child-and-baby self and then confronted with the endangering mother as she herself had experienced her. She suffered considerable pain and anxiety. But she eventually began to believe that the analysis was really for her and that I was available for her as a person in her own right, and that indeed she was a person who had an existence and a value quite apart from her functions as mother, teacher, housewife or scapegoat.

Initially, Mrs X had put a great deal of her own childhood self into Barbara. This had led to confusion in Barbara and cut Mrs X off from her own roots. She could gain access to the helpless, angry and frightened part of herself only at the price of exposing herself to the pain and conflicts that she had experienced in her own childhood, a risk that she only dared take when she could trust me to stand by her without in any way abusing the situation. By liberating her own encapsulated child, she made available to herself those qualities which, as I said in my introduction, are characteristic of childhood, namely, flexibility, curiosity, a general responsiveness and the willingness to grow.

Towards the end of her analysis Mrs X was able to recognize that children at different stages in their development need 'looking after' in different ways. Indeed, when her love of children had become less absolute and obsessive, some of her other needs also emerged. She found renewed satisfaction in her sexual relations with her husband, in housework and in gardening as well as her relationship with Barbara.

What was so impressive about Mrs X was that she could be analysed; that she was capable of so much unconscious co-operation. And in spite of her age, situation, appearance and the severity of her paedophilic desires, she proved to be flexible and able to change and to develop. Admittedly, her general restlessness, several near mental breakdowns and her religious searchings had been signs that her suffering was near the surface. But her restlessness was also deep enough to lead her to attempt to break the matriarchal tie that had bound so many generations already.

3

The Scope and Dimensions of Paedophilia

Kenneth Lambert

I

PAEDOPHILIA IN EVERYDAY LIFE

THE CASE OF PAUL

Paul, who is married and the father of an adolescent boy and a pre-pubertal girl, is good-looking, lively and youthful. He is a lover of beauty in art, nature and young women. He is able in business, adventurous and talented and although he avoids conflict, he can be ruthless in delivering the *coup de grâce* to unsuccessful enterprises. His problem ranges round his lack of depth and a barely recognized sense of depression and despair. He begins new projects with enthusiasm but after a while becomes disillusioned so that the project is abandoned or used as a stepping-stone to another and 'improved' venture. His flexibility and business acumen are invaluable to him at work and, while the economy was expanding, he was able to seize opportunities and make quick profits. Unlike his partners and bosses, it is only too easy for him to realize that there is a limit to the amount of work which yields worthwhile results. He dislikes making great efforts and tries to maximize his leisure time.

Through this flair, he was able to compensate for a stuffy, cramped and fussed-over childhood and the depression that resulted from his parents' broken marriage. A lively boy, he had been over-cossetted and kept too clean by his mother who had remarried and seems to have felt guilty for the narcissistic self-absorbtion that had caused her, when young, to somewhat neglect her baby. She seems to have spent her later years trying to make up for this neglect, unfortunately at unsuitable periods in Paul's development. His father, with whom he spent a very short time in his childhood and youth and who lived in another country, appeared to Paul to be a thoroughgoing egotist. He never remarried and seems to have exploited his mistress quite successfully while neglecting his son, depriving him emotionally by long absence, and financially when it came to providing support for his higher education and his initial business enterprise. From Paul's point of view, his father appeared to be only really interested in his own business, in securing domestic care from his self-sufficient mistress, and in hunting, shooting and dogs. Thus the boy grew up—without brothers or sisters.

This emotionally unsatisfactory background brought out various traits in Paul. The inevitable underlying anger, depression and loneliness undermined his educational and learning processes and, indeed, most of his activities. He was able to cope because of his ability to muster a cheerful appearance, a likeable manner and a passion for adventure. He had something of the classical hero about him and, in Jung's terms, the image and feeling of the *puer aeternus*, the everlasting youth, seemed to possess him. This lonely, rather loveless, experience drove him into the search for beauty. The 'stuffing', over-protective attitude both of his mother and of his new undynamic step-father impelled him at the age of eighteen, through sheer boredom and depression, to persuade them to help him leave home and seek adventure and further education abroad. The absent father was, in a way, replaced or rather, rendered perpetually present by Paul's unconsciously living a life that was similar in many essential aspects to the life lived by his father. Despite important differences, Paul's life was markedly an egotistical existence of a 'do-it-yourself' or 'go-it-alone' sort. Because of his secret hatred for his parents he kept family involvement minimal and substituted a multiplicity of erotic, sporting and recreational activities, largely of an effortless sort.

Yet there was a difference, arising perhaps from a feeling, not quite successfully warded off, of what it is like to be an emotionally starved child. He married a woman from a more closely-knit though somewhat unstable family. It was not very long, though, before the marriage as well as the children became disturbed. Both Paul and his wife, however, unlike the earlier generation, were able to seek analytic help. During the course of this, Paul discovered, side by side with the same sense of the irksomeness of family commitments so noticeable in his father, another dimension of feeling. This was an enjoyment of his children: a deeper recognition of the needs they had of him as a father and a satisfaction in meeting them thus. Furthermore, this potential for enjoying parenthood developed in a relatively unsentimental way, balanced as it was by the remnants of the wish for a playboy existence that arose out of the adolescent aspects of his nature.

Nevertheless, that this new type of loving maintained itself without petering out caused me to wonder how this could have come about in a person whose emotional background had been so unfavourable. The answer must be that his background could not have been totally bleak. His mother, though initially unprepared for motherhood, became more capable of caring as time went on and did set him free at the age of eighteen, for which he was grateful. Furthermore, the rather good-looking boy became, as a young man, the recipient of a good deal of love and affection from girlfriends and older men and later from his wife, although his relationships often ended abruptly. Prior to his experience of my care, he had responded uncynically to the concern and empathy of a woman analyst. So Paul's life had not been as loveless as it appeared on the surface and his cynicism and brittleness of feeling were by no means absolute. His capacity for parental loving developed despite the boredom and underlying hatred for his mother-wife (indeed all mothers) and children that had its clear origin in his early life.

One day he told me a dream which both intrigued and troubled him. He dreamt that he was on the back seat of a limousine with a young girl aged eight or ten who was reminiscent of his daughter. The girl was naked and began to make sexual advances. Intercourse was quite easy. Paul was astonished that this was possible with so young and small a girl. As he talked about the dream he remembered that he had read that Masai girls began sexual intercourse at the age of ten. He also remembered, suddenly, a man who had told him that he had had regular sexual intercourse with his own daughter and was becoming rather worried about it. It became clear, as Paul talked, that his incestuous paedophilic feelings towards his own daughter had become repressed and unconscious. As is probably the case with most people, Paul recognized incestuous feelings in others more easily than in himself, until fairly clear evidence came out in the dream containing images of impulses normally dissociated from consciousness. He began to see how he was distorting reality and how dangerous it was to blind himself to the incestuous link with his daughter. Repressed incestuous feelings often express themselves negatively through neglect or even cruelty towards a child with the unconscious aim of making them as unthinkable as they are unrealizable. It also became clearer that Paul's roving eye for young beauties was motivated, in part at least, by repressed incestuous wishes both for his mother, who had been a beauty when he was a little boy, and for his own daughter. Another point which emerged spontaneously in discussion centred round the dream image of his young daughter's readiness for intercourse and his surprise at her ability. This made him realize that he had been blinding himself to her growth towards adolescence and her need for his recognition of her as in essence a potentially satisfactory sexual female, able to relate with her peers at a later phase of her life. The withholding of this kind of fathering, which the dream showed him to be in danger of doing, tends to cause young women to seek substitutes for it in boyfriends, lovers and husbands, thus introducing strains that can be harmful, even disastrous, to

83

fulfilment in marital, maternal and other relationships.

Of course, Paul's holding back from his daughter, as well as from the rest of the family, may have been due to lack of any effective confirmation of his male identity in his own youth. Thus, the woman analyst with whom he had formerly worked for a short time wrote to me of his possessing a number of excellent qualities that had been hampered or unrealized as a result both of his early environment and of his adult life which was of a kind that a person so deprived might unconsciously seek for himself. The people he worked with during his early manhood tended to confirm the cynical, shallow, heartless and despairing qualities of his nature rather than the positive ones. Accordingly, the problems of Paul's personality as such, rather than those concerning his relationship with his daughter, show that the dream we have been discussing can be understood in a still deeper way as depicting the therapeutic experiences begun with his woman analyst and continued by me.

One of the features of Paul's psychology was that he complained of being unable to commit himself deeply to any relationship. He was very conscious of this and upset by it. He felt that he had not fully realized his potential. He was not completely locked up in his blind unconscious superficiality, a superficiality made tolerable by sustaining himself in a state of excitement through business coups, erotic adventures and constant changes of scenery, job and habitat. He knew enough of the long-term damage to his emotional life to seek the help of an analyst.[1] Thus Paul was sufficiently in earnest about his treatment to be able to tolerate the analysis of his defensive attempts to keep his analyst at arm's length; his defensive incredulousness (compared with genuine puzzle-

[1] Very often, repair in analysis can be achieved through an investigation into what is generally called transference. The patient begins to treat the analyst in the same way as he has always treated parents, siblings and intimate friends—indeed anyone with whom a relationship might be formed. He transfers memories of and experiences with people important in his past or present on to his analyst and treats him as if he were one of them.

ment) over some of his analyst's interpretations; his defensive thought blockages; his defensive fear of the couch; his defensive need to keep his eyes fixed upon the analyst's face so that he could continually scan the expression on it.

In the light of these observations it is possible to understand the dream as an image of the development in his feelings towards his analyst. If the eight- or ten-year-old daughter figure is taken to represent something in himself, then things become much clearer. It is the daughter figure in him which can allow himself to feel something for the analyst and to allow him to penetrate his being. It represents a 'coming to life' for him behind the scenes.

It is taking place in the background of his psyche (the back seats in the limousine) and it surprises him. Analytically speaking, the figure of his daughter represents his deeply repressed but natural homosexual feeling for his father which, owing to the sporadic nature of their relationship, had never really been given a chance.

To stunt passive homosexual feelings for a father can have serious repercussions upon a boy's emotional development and can produce unsatisfying yearning-rebellious feelings towards male authority. It throws the boy back upon the mother, who then has to carry too great an emotional load. It can hamper the boy's ability to accept and learn from his father much that would enable him to achieve a sense of male identity. It robs him of the feeling of being sexually accepted by his father and, in the case of Paul, it had hindered his ability to give a sense of sexual acceptance to his daughter. This acceptance does not involve actual sexual acts but does have a basis in sexual feelings and appreciation. In the light of this, we may say that Paul had reached an important moment in his life. He had the opportunity at last to work through into consciousness his passive homosexual feelings— not with his father, but with the analyst who is in place of the father. In other words he was at a point where he could experience not only his own emotional needs but also those of his daughter. Thus the two approaches to the dream, one from the point of view of outer relationship and the other from the point of view of his inner life, turn out to be complementary and mutually interactive.

The situation depicted in the dream was, roughly speaking, beginning to show in Paul's relationship with me. From being formal, polite and highly selective in what he chose to communicate, he became more spontaneous, candid and confiding. Having initially used an easy charm upon me, he was beginning to show more commitment and unqualified trust. Side by side with his release into greater spontaneity, small but significant events were taking place in his outer life.

One day he told me a delightful story. The previous evening, at home, his young daughter had actually made the proposition to him and his wife that it was high time that she (the daughter) shared her father's bed for once. Mother, she said, had had plenty of opportunities and should now stand down as she (the daughter) was beginning to grow up. Paul was not unprepared for this, coming as it did quite soon after the dream, and so he and his wife could handle the announcement sympathetically. They indicated to her that it was natural that as she grew up she would begin to think that it was her turn to be like mother, and that feelings of rivalry with her mother were to be expected. It would not be true rivalry, however, to have her father, but rather to have someone of her own in due course. But it was an understandable need to know that her father approved of her as she grew into a woman. Such a reply was logical and helpful though it seems likely that the daughter's direct request sprang from a deep doubt as to whether she was sufficiently accepted by her father as a female. This doubt had probably been experienced with such urgency that it gave her the impulse to break through the barrier in a concrete way. As the same time, by laying her request openly before her parents, she seems really to have ensured that what she requested would *not* take place, but might be understood.

A month later, Paul was again approached—this time by a couple of male students on behalf of a student girlfriend of theirs. She had seen Paul, and despatched the two students to ask him whether he, as a mature man, would consider initiating her further into the experience of sex. This request was sympathetically refused by Paul. He considered the action inappropriate—symptomatic of a problem rather than likely to lead to creative growth. Furthermore Paul found that he was not really tempted.

I have chosen this simple account of Paul's situation as a suitable centre round which to collect a number of points which illustrate paedophilia in everyday life. I do not claim that this story is in any way peculiar or special. It is true that, at a deep level, Paul's story is that of a man in whom the early interaction between himself and his environment hindered the development of his emotional life. As is often the case, his initial impulse to seek analytical help arose from difficulties in his marriage and family. Marriage and children began to reveal afresh and activate stresses arising from flaws and weaknesses in childhood development that are often obscured during the vigorous years of early adulthood. Paul's story is, therefore, in principle fairly common—apart from his unusual step in seeking analytical help—and might almost represent a cultural style in many circles. To the extent however that this is so, the style involved is open to criticism from the angle of emotional fulfilment. Fortunately we are still in an area where there is hope of improvement and renewal as a result of analytical investigation, and perhaps Paul's story illustrates some elements of hope.

THE ETYMOLOGY OF THE WORD 'PAEDOPHILIA'

In assessing the contribution of Paul's story to the subject of paedophilia, I propose, after dealing with the emotions aroused by the word, to do what always seems useful when handling a word used in psychology, namely to consider its etymology. This is particularly important in dealing with a word as emotive as paedophilia. Traditionally the average citizen reacts with horror to the whole idea. He thinks of it mainly in terms of the sexual seduction by adults of children and adolescents, sometimes accompanied by violence or even death. When he reads the saddening accounts of it reported in newspapers, he is outraged and grieves for the child and his parents, while he regards the offending adult and his motives as totally alien to anything he can understand or even want to understand. If he is an inmate of a prison, he will be cruel to sex offenders against young children. These primitive feeling-reactions are understandable provided they do not lead to cruel action. It is dangerous to undermine such feelings rather than inform them, even though they are psychologically suspect and determined by many unconscious considerations. Nevertheless, they need supplementing by the recognition that paedophilia, in both its positive and its destructive forms, is to be found in most people in some form or other, and that the paedophilic offender receives the projection of this often-disapproved feature of the human psyche. It is also true that the destructive perversions of it by which it is best known represent a type of illness the roots of which are beginning to be understood analytically in terms of early development. Such a recognition naturally has a chastening effect upon reasonably self-aware people especially if they find themselves very emotionally disturbed by and sadistically inclined towards paedophilic offenders. (It ought to be added that to be entirely unmoved or to take it lightly is equally suspect.) Such a recognition can become the motive power for increased awareness that the human tragedy involved is real and embraces not only the young victim and his family but the adult offender as well. Finally, another factor has emerged, confusing emotionally, though without much logical justification. It is now realized that the young victims often appear to be themselves much more emotionally involved than had previously been thought. Therefore, the idea has grown up that it is less and less clear who is the victim—the young person or the adult. Such an idea is, in fact, only plausible when the adult involved is psychotic and emotionally younger than the young person involved. Such a person becomes fair game for any ruthless youngster. Otherwise the responsibility still rests with the adult.

Facts like these have produced in some quarters an almost emotive swing away from the ordinary citizen's horror at paedophilic abuse. As is the case with attitudes towards many forms of sexual deviance, the swing starts with the recognition that a pathological element may be involved, although this is not carefully defined. But as time goes on, questioning minds begin to inquire whether there is, in the last resort, any pathological element at all, and they begin to regard sexual deviations quite simply as alternative ways of living, with nothing more to be said about them. It is the fear, not wholly unjustified, of serious legal persecution of sexual deviants that tempts people to minimize the problems involved by shallow and rationalistic thinking, especially in the case of paedophilia. It would involve throwing overboard the results of much painstaking research into the human developmental process as well as discounting the significance of the ordinary citizen's sense of unease over this type of deviance.

We can, however, employ the emotion aroused in such controversies to rethink and study the whole subject. Starting afresh involves considering the etymology of the word paedophilia, for etymology involves origins. The Greek words involved are *paidos* and *philia*. *Pais*, *paidos*, meaning a child, is familiar in words like paediatrics, pedagogy and pederasty. In English usage today, only the medical term, paediatrics, has taken on a descriptive meaning that carries an undertone of commendation. The other two words carry pejorative undertones. The word *philia*, on the other hand, emerged in the Greek language out of a general group of words all translated into English as love. This group included *eros*, *philia*, and *agape*, all used interchangeably, if not indiscriminately, in earlier Greek literature. Before psychology got to work on love and split it up into a number of distinct connotations, i.e. *eros* (sexuality), *philia* (affection) and *agape* (esteem and respect), it was acknowledged that they were all present in

89

different degrees, forms and modes of expression in varying personal relationships. As greater discrimination developed, *philia* was generally used in contexts where the emphasis rested more upon warm loving family affection, the love between master and slave, or the love between gods and men. There seemed always to have been an element of responsibility involved; that of parents, elders and teachers towards the young; of masters towards slaves, of gods towards men. Nevertheless, something of a darker, more instinctual, more metaphysical undercurrent is also involved. In the original less differentiated meaning of the word, however, the emphasis upon responsibility alone would probably not have been made at the expense of either sexual elements or respect and esteem. Thus when we consider how rich the original meaning of love was, it would be unrealistic to blind ourselves to the fact that inherent in it can be found the seeds of deep conflict, especially in the immensely limited conditions of the human situation within which love arises. There are clashes between sexuality, affection, respect and esteem. There is a clash between the passion for the inner development of the individual psyche and the claims and fulfilments of personal and social relationships within the family and other groups within which it finds itself and without whom its whole meaning is diminished. There is the clash between the wish for fusionary states of identity on the one hand and separateness on the other. There is the clash between the drive towards incest and the pull away from the family. Finally there is the tension between the inner reality of man and the outer reality of his world.

It was because of the complexity of man's situation and the growing failure of the traditional patterns and mores to accommodate this, together with the resultant sense of dis-ease among individuals, that the analytical schools arose. Freud's effort was to integrate man's divided psyche by re-directing our attention to the complexities of the multi-dimensional sexuality that lies at the foundation of human relationships. Jung was to uncover the incestuous elements that lay behind our cultural and religious life and to draw our attention to archetypal forces operating from within the psyche in ways that could be benign or malign, creative or totally destructive to individual life. Klein was to explore the unconscious fantasies of early childhood in all the passionate vigour of its imagery. The English analysts, Winnicott and Fordham, have explored the inter-relationship between the inner world of childhood and the outer personal environment provided by mother, father, family, school and community. Furthermore, the whole analytic endeavour during the present century has included the vitally necessary task of uncovering the unconscious dark potential in love—the hatred, rivalry and tyranny that increase in intensity the more idealized the love becomes.

Against this background, we may return to the meaning covered by the word paedophilia. We can see that what is involved is a warm, loving affection towards a child in relation to whom a certain responsibility is felt and undertaken. These particular qualities of love are focused on, and stand against, a general background of erotic and sexual feeling coupled with respect and esteem. That the paedophilic impulse can now also be seen to carry an undercurrent of tendencies which have, during most of our cultural history, been frowned upon when displayed is one of the achievements of analytical endeavour. Thus sexual possessiveness, envy, resentment, competitiveness, even discouragement and hatred of the young are also unconsciously present in the paedophilic drive. These shadow qualities, when recognized and contained, often play a meaningful and constructive part in the care of the young. When unconscious, however, they can lead to thoroughly destructive results, not only in adults who are unaware of the issues involved in parenthood and teaching, but also in those who are keen to be good parents and pride themselves on it. Among members of this last group, the darker sides can sometimes work in subtle, almost invisible ways that secretly undermine their consciously good intentions and breed resentment in the young, a fact especially puzzling to those parents who feel they have done so much for their children.

POSITIVE AND NEGATIVE ASPECTS OF
PAEDOPHILIA IN EVERYDAY LIFE

The paedophilic impulse, when described in these fuller terms, can provide the soundest psychological environment within which the young can develop in an individual and creative way. If we were to spell out the considerations involved, they would be along the following lines. First, the sexual element, in which incestuous sexuality plays an important part, stimulates the adult involved to focus attention upon the young specifically in his or her care. This can make the adult creative and imaginative in understanding and satisfying the inner needs of the young. It can enable him to act as a receptor and container for them in their experimentation and in their attempts to come to grips with their lives. Secondly, the warm affection gives many children a favourable psychological climate within which they can be sufficiently relaxed to learn and grow. Thirdly, the responsible aspect of paedophilia gives the adults the opportunity of being steady, reliable and enduring at a time when the child or young person is extremely dependent on their remaining 'an alive and available presence'.[2] Fourthly, the esteem element helps the adult to respect the growing individuality and true emergent self of the younger person in his care.

Apart from these four positive points, the dark sides can be used positively where the adult is conscious and mature enough (i.e., has enough ego-strength) to be able to handle them. First, the sexual possessiveness can, if handled properly, provide enough focus in the adult for him to feel securely that he or she is dealing with 'my child', 'my pupil', etc. For a child to have a sense of belonging makes all the difference to growth, learning and environment. Secondly, envy of the young by adults can become subtly destructive to all concerned. For instance, subtle injustices towards children, often

[2] D. W. Winnicott, *The Integration Process and the Facilitating Environment* (Hogarth Press and the Institute of Psychoanalysis 1965), pp. 77-8.

under the guise of good intentions, result in unconscious depressions and guilt feelings in the envious adults. These latter feelings can then lead to further subtle malpractice. On the other hand, if envy is recognized and contained, it can be turned into a source of emulation and stimulation. Adults responsible for the young may be stimulated by envy into maintaining freshness and flexibility of mind. This increases the adults' understanding of the young, thus helping their growth and educational needs, and provides adults with one of the benefits of maturity. Thirdly, adults often feel competitive and have a tendency to 'slap down' children. These tendencies, operating unconsciously, or even as a conscious policy of action, are rightly to be deplored. Even here, however, adults who can consciously control these impulses can employ them to provide something hard for the young person to fight against, thereby stretching his resources and enabling him to discover hitherto unrealized powers. Fourthly, the hatred which exists on the underside of love and which results from the restrictions on adult freedom in child care can also be turned to constructive account. It can curb the tendency of some adults to swamp the young with care and concern and hence to deprive them of that breathing space so essential for life, growth and learning, the lack of which is cramping and painful to the ardent spirit.

This short account of ways in which the dark side of the paedophilic impulse may be integrated might appear to be rather idealized and, indeed, so positive and good as to represent a dubious preparation of the young for the difficulties of life. This criticism may be just in principle; in practice, it is less likely to be relevant. In the first place, it is important that the young are only gradually introduced to the full rigours and dangers of adult life. They need some protection while they are growing. In the second place, despite all conscious efforts in adults, the shadow tends not to be very consistently or satisfactorily integrated. Thus the young are unlikely to be over-protected against difficult environments and will find plenty to complain about and struggle with. Finally, it is important to realize that what we are dealing with is not an ideal but a phenomenon, namely paedophilia, which is a spontaneous feeling and certainly not a moral aim.

The way in which paedophilia has been described here plainly presents a syndrome of qualities that represent a rather mature attitude. The normal human lot works out in a much more rough and ready way. Ordinary human beings find themselves married and with children as a result of all sorts of forces, many of them unconscious. Often, young parents carry within themselves sketchy memories, many of them painful, of their own experiences as children. Many of them are in rebellion against what happened to them at the hands of their parents and teachers and have sworn that they will not subject any children of theirs to such an 'awful upbringing'. Others, when dealing with their own children, blindly expect to repeat with little change what happened to them when they were young. Again, there are those who found their upbringing good enough and seem reasonably at ease amongst the difficulties of caring for children. They react instinctively to their children's needs and spontaneously improve upon their own upbringing where possible. Today we know, however, that there are some who, at a deep level, are tempted to reject the whole situation of family life and to deny the reality or value of this kind of unit. They adopt ways of life that are thought to be viable alternatives, if not tremendously exciting improvements, upon anything hitherto thought of or experienced.

I hope that at this point, apart from a description of the dynamics and origins of paedophilia, I have adequately described its influence as a positive force in everyday life.

We must now re-examine the story of Paul and show how his development was hampered by what may be called the defective paedophilic situation in his early environment and schooldays. This examination should illustrate further some of the dynamic aspects of the paedophilic impulse which have not been covered so far by our descriptions of its content, and the impact of the impulse upon the growth and educational processes in children and young people.

In considering Paul's case, we are brought up against a situation which must have been in existence before he was born, or at any rate, very early in his life, namely defects in his parents' marriage which in fact collapsed when he was very young. Analysts have been forced by the plight of many patients to consider the marriage situation into which they were born and which constituted the environment within which they grew up. It is well known among analysts that the oedipal situation is best managed when the sexual and erotic relationship between the parents is sound. The children are then spared the extra stress that arises if the unsatisfied sexuality of one or both parents devolves upon them. They are then able to make the necessary identifications with the parent of the same sex and go on to establish their own sexual identity. Furthermore, the work of Klein and her followers has established that what they call 'the primal scene' is central to the emotional wellbeing of children. The primal scene is the essential relationship between mother and father. Put into terms of early infantile fantasy, in which certain parts of the body represent the whole persons of the parents, the primal scene includes among many things the relationship between breast and penis, experienced in oral terms; or, at a later date, between vagina and penis. The fantasies are influenced by what the child may think he observes going on. When the relationship is reasonably good, the fantasy is that the breast and penis are life-giving to both parents and children, and that the penis makes good the flow of babies inside the mother, so that her generosity is available to the family, and in general the mother's insides are kept sound and good. Thus a model of the marriage relationship is established as a result of the interaction between what the child thinks he perceives and his inner expectations and hopes—archetypal expectations as Jung would put it. This model unconsciously determines the growing person's expectations of marriage when he enters upon it. Paul's primal scene experience was of a marriage between a narcissistic and self-absorbed woman and an egotistical man, where the primal scene was broken up, so that it was never experienced as a life-giving situation where Paul could be nourished and developed by the positive paedophilic impulses of his parents. At best the mother was a 'stuffing' one, abandoned by an unconcerned father. She later married Paul's step-father who made no attempt to make his presence felt other than by satisfying her whims and fancies. They had no further children and in this situation there was no place for children or even for an only child like Paul.

It is well known that the only child is plagued by loneliness, which he fears, and by a longing for siblings, which he also fears. He is worried by the belief that he has killed all the babies inside the mother and is demoralized and guilty at the thought that he is a murderer. Paul's childhood feelings seem almost certainly to have been of this sort. He was preoccupied and did not learn as well as his abilities would suggest was possible. He was depressed and angry. And he had little self-esteem, as he had been starved of the paedophilic attention which his parents could not give him. Without a model of the primal pair who gave themselves to each other, he could not give himself to work or study in depth. When he married he was still unconsciously influenced by the model of a selfishly demanding mother and a father who absented himself from business and pleasure and found the whole set-up of marriage and family an irksome tie. Even at school, he found no life-giving paedophilic teachers. The lessons were formal and examination-orientated. There was little in the way of personal interaction with the teachers. He did not find himself much involved in the *amor paedagogicus* situation (where the teacher has love for his pupils), thus missing the experience so vividly described by Plato in which the homosexual love of boys exerted such an important cultural influence at the time when the old gods and social mores were failing and a new level of consciousness was dawning. Thus his whole maturation process, conceived of in terms of growth, learning and the acquiring of skills, was hampered in profound but subtle ways. Those real abilities which he did develop he

96

did not regard as anything more than half-hearted achievements. They were the result of a compromise between the need to earn money by work and the pull of a kind of inertia that was more attracted to play. He had little respect for his abilities, or for anything that he did, or on the whole for the ability of the people around him.

It does not require too much imagination to become involved in Paul's plight. Underneath the pleasant, easy exterior, there was an emotional desert and a continual underlying depression that diminished the amount of energy available. This meant that he never gained the satisfaction of achievement through effort and concentration. If we ask where the energy went to, we find that it was being employed as follows:

First, in worrying about the non-productivity of the parents. These are parents 'inside' Paul. Analysts call them internal objects. They are formed by a mixture of actual experiences of parents and the images of them that seem to be innately ready to be activated. Thus an experience of the absent father matches one of the many archetypal expectations that children have of the kind of father they may meet, in this case the absent, non-creative father. For Paul, this meant that he was saddled with an inner feeling that the father part of his nature was absent and non-creative. Analysts call this the situation of having an internal father of an absent and non-creative sort. Paul had a deep worry about his own creativity as a result of the non-creative internal parents.

Secondly, in wondering how to alleviate the mental and emotional pain of feeling alone in a world where there is no real place for him and no one to love and justify him. Paul could not find this experience anywhere.

Thirdly, engaging in activity designed to drown the depressed feelings. These activities, generally called 'manic defence activities', give an artificial feeling of life, love and creativity through the excitement they engender.

When Paul was a boy, he used to employ his native sense of humour in a whole range of merry pranks and tricks both at school and among other boys in the streets. He could get excitement out of disobeying his mother's instructions and getting mixed up in fights and scuffles that made him dirty and dishevelled. He also got a thrill out of not being found out and maintaining a poker face. As he grew up, the thrills were obtained by business adventures together with all sorts of erotic, sexual, recreational and travel consolations and the excitements connected with constantly breaking up old situations and seeking new ones. Then again, he sought the beauty of the good, generous breast and vagina of the mother, and the good, healing and creative penis of the father, both of which he had missed, in the beauty of young girls, in art, in craftsmanship and in the company of artists and craftsmen. Often the image was confused with the substance and the outer form with the inner reality. All this utilized considerable energy, not in creatively satisfying work and personal relationships and family, but in rendering tolerable his emotional desert and inner sense of despair.

Paul had no experience of being on the receiving end of the paedophilic impulse. He had never benefited from its positive life-giving aspects and so it was not easy for him to appreciate it, let alone get much of a paedophilic feeling in relation to children. This included the child or children of his own inner world. Even when he had become interested in philosophy, Jungian psychology and eastern religion, long before he sought analysis, these interests did not help repair the early damage. They represented additional variants on his manic defences against depression, and held out the promise of obtaining magical consolation now that he was getting older and 'tied down' by family responsibilities.

THE BASIS OF THE FAMILY IN THE PRIMAL SCENE

Despite Paul's manic expenditure of energy on substitutes, his deep-rooted and unconscious energy-consuming preoccupation was to repair the damaged primal scene that had so hindered his development. For many people, this basis for their life works well enough for them to be able to take it for granted.

They certainly do not have constantly to use up energy investigating, exploring and shoring up the foundations of their whole existence, let alone expend it upon frantic defence. So for them there is enough vigour available for a creative life. The importance of the primal scene to the whole subject of paedophilia can hardly be exaggerated. As first described by Freud and elaborated by Melanie Klein, the primal scene is marked by five participants: the two parents, the boy, the girl and the baby-inside-the-mother. This is an internal fantasy expectation that seems to be inherent in the young child psyche both in children and in adults. While corresponding to a typical moment in the life of families, this also describes some of the make-up of the inner world of man. Here we have the interpenetrating copulation of mother and father, the male and female children (or young and growing parts), and the pregnant or potentially pregnant mother full of babies. In this setting love and hate, co-operation and rivalry, creativity, life, death, violence, repair, envy and jealousy all jostle together. Indeed, where the paedophilic drives are sound enough this rich admixture of emotion represents a positive force for growth. However, when the dynamics of the outer or inner family become unsatisfactory, non-life-giving, and even destructive, persecuted depression begins to take over. At this stage, to quote Donald Meltzer: 'we must make an additional augmentation. A sixth figure enters upon the scene: the "outsider", the stranger to the family, the enemy of parental creativity, of love; the evil one, the cynic, the spoiler, the carrier of the mark of Cain'.[3] This outsider attitude, the cynical hostility towards the family, is not an uncommon style of life. Indeed it is almost a cult in the outer world of society today. In the case of Paul, it operated mainly as a negative internal figure. He had become cynical and despairing about parental figures and family situations. With superficial amiability he could quote innumerable public figures who had been corrupt in their social functioning as parent-figures in society. He knew relations, in-laws, friends and colleagues who were cynically neglectful

[3] Donald Meltzer, *Sexual States of Mind* (Clurie Press 1973), p. 90.

of their children or the people under their care. He knew of physicians and analysts who betrayed their patients. He despaired of the child within himself ever finding worth-while meaningful experiences, or of ever being able to get a feeling of value with which to persevere into the mastery of work or the achievement of excellence of any sort. There was in Paul an envy of good family experiences which worked itself out in depression and the quest of excitement. The envy sought to destroy familial creative goodness—in his case by making him disbelieve in its existence—both in the external world and also in his own inner world. He therefore thought that the anti-family mode of life was superior, more satisfying and more exhilarating and enriching. His attitude contained a hidden negativism whereby the good was denied and called evil. In Meltzer's view, the origins of sadistic (destructive) perverse sexual states of mind lie in this deep disturbance of feeling and emotion. Indeed, it is arguable that the real significance of sexual perversions lies much more in the emotive quality behind them than in the acts themselves. The negativism of the perversion, to quote Meltzer again,

wills to create a world which is the negative of everything in nature, in the realm of good objects. The impulses are therefore fundamentally anti-nature and the world it seeks to build is the world of the life-less, for whom the great anxieties of the living, time-bound, cannot exist. The emotive quality of sadistic perverse sexual states of mind is therefore basically manic. It is not the sensuality that is lusted after but the triumphant abolition of depressive and even persecutory anxiety—depressive above all.[4]

In the use of the word 'sadistic' Meltzer is here referring to the situation where the destructive part of the self has seized the whole of the personality.

As we have seen, Paul's problem was not intractably severe. He had never even considered taking up the perverse and

[4] Op. cit., p. 92.

negativistic forms of paedophilia on the grossly concrete level. He was rather the subtle victim in his inner life of the paedophilic failure of his earlier environment. Furthermore, without quite knowing why, he was never satisfied with the form of his life and when he started analysis he persevered with it. We may leave him here—with gratitude for having helped to shed light on some subtle forms of the phenomena we are studying.

II

SOME PERVERSIONS OF PAEDOPHILIA IN FANTASY AND ACTION

A PERVERSE PAEDOPHILIC FANTASY

I now move on to a short examination of the way in which the perverse or negativistic type of paedophilia works out in terms of human experience. This can take several forms. Probably the most common form is that of a luxuriant fantasy life, in which sexual ecstasy with child or pubescent sexual partners predominates, together with the thrills of subterfuge and the hoodwinking of parental authorities and horrible mothers. There is evidence to make us suspect that fantasies of this sort are not always conscious and that it may be a by-product of pornography to bring them to consciousness by forming and focusing on relevant themes. The less common form—at the other end of the spectrum—is simply an acting out of such fantasies, accompanied by intense sexual excitement, through the straightforward seduction of the young into sexual activity. If we consider the fantasy-laden life which is depicted in semi-pornographic literature, we can find expression of the paedophilic fantasy that almost exactly accords with the phenomena described by Meltzer under the heading of the negativistic paedophilia perversion. One such book is given the highly descriptive but ambivalent title of *Green Fruit.*[5] This purports to be the detailed account of the author's

[5] A forthcoming publication from Grove Press, New York.

paedophilic life, particularly during the few years when he was practising paedophilia prior to his imprisonment for it. There is an introduction by a psychologist in which the scientific interest of the account is stressed and a description given of the author. It is of less interest for our purposes to consider the authenticity of the book than to examine it simply as a piece of fantasy of a negativistic perverse paedophilic sort.

The author opens the story of his sexual adventures by reporting that when he was a youth at sea he was violently buggered by a grown man. The experience was marked by overwhelming sensations, the quintessence of pain and violent excitement. After this opening storm of homosexual experience the author later settled ashore, married and took up photography. It was not very long before he found his wife boring and physically loathsome. As his only daughter reached the threshold of puberty he planned, and succeeded, in seducing her. After a considerable degree of resistance, she surrendered to violent intercourse (just as he had, when young) and was reduced to obedience and co-operation with him in pornographic photography. His scorned wife did not, however, fully oppose what was going on. After a time, the daughter began to break away and acquired a boyfriend whom she finally married. Enraged, the author went on to seduce other prepubescent girls. He chose friends of his daughter and their sisters and went in for group sex, accompanied by photography. It was not long before the daughter's marriage broke down. She returned, a soured person, to keep house for her father who was now alone. And, while she lived in his house, she had to tolerate his paedophilic activity with a succession of young girls. These adventures finally ended when the author was betrayed, charged and imprisoned.

These are simply the bare bones of the action in the perverse fantasy of the author. There was a psychic accompaniment to it, however, that is important for understanding negativistic paedophilic perversion. If we consider the body feelings experienced by the author and the feelings he wished to induce in the young girls, we find, in line with Meltzer's description

102

quoted above, little in the way of sensuality and love. This fact could perhaps unconsciously be in line with the title of his book *Green Fruit*. What we do find in the book are many expressions of intense excitement which purport to verge on ecstasy. First, there are feelings about wives and mothers; for instance, he enjoys enraging, taunting and scorning his wife. He enjoys making up to the mothers of the young girls he seduces. Often, after he has got the young girls to persuade their mothers to let them stay the weekend with him for photographic sessions, he finally gets the mothers to the point of asking him to have the young girls to stay. He finds it exciting that the mothers know so little about their daughters' goings-on with him. Then again he often writes with a shudder about mothers and wives. They fill him with horror and loathing. They are 'old bags' and there is a sense of sadistic excitement in ensuring that they are humiliated and shunned.

Secondly, he finds it tremendously stimulating to seduce his daughter and other young girls. That will pay the mothers back. There is no mention of the fathers anywhere. His daughter is to be quite different from her mother. She is to be the one with a beautiful, smooth, slim body. Her immature breasts are not to be pendulant and shapeless like her mother's. She is to be beautifully free from pubic hair and her genitals will be like a rosebud. She is not to become like her mother but will remain Daddy's daughter. He will give her exquisite sexual satisfaction and that's what she will be for. It is the same with the other young girls—the friends and sisters. They are also to be saved from their mothers. He is to be the purveyor of a new sexual ecstasy.

Thirdly, there is a discussion of the great excitement he feels in exerting his power over his daughter and the other girls. He wishes to reduce his daughter, for instance, to a state of complete sexual obedience to him. Thus, after seducing her, he says, with triumphant authority: 'Now you must be a good girl and promise to obey me in every detail of life absolutely.' Likewise he exults in the power he has over other young girls. Having sexually stimulated them to the greatest possible degree

103

and transmitted his excited state to them, he reduced them to pleading with him to ease their unbearable sexual tension and revels in their desperate dependence upon him. And with what sense of 'potency' does he, the full-grown man, penetrate deeply the sexually immature pubertal girls. Thus he will overcome the dreaded power of the mothers. He will humiliate, scorn and offend them; he will seek to break the mother-daughter relationship; he will substitute for the mother, a daughter whom he can dominate because of her immaturity—unlike her bossy mother.

Fourthly, even with this degree of acted out 'overcoming' of the mother, he still demonstrated a considerable residue of fear of her (the mother) and of the primal scene. This was shown by his excitement of voyeurism and photography. The author loved to photograph sexual intercourse and the genitals of the young girls. In other words, he liked to view the primal scene 'from a distance', to look at immature female bodies from a point not too close at hand. Thus, group sex between him and several girls, with one taking photographs, was particularly exciting because of his profound fear of sexuality and, in particular, of the mother's body which it was dangerous to get near because of its horrible fascination.

The intense psychic excitements so far described are not particularly sensual. Full of homosexual content, they are connected with (a) punishing the mother—and also the father who is entirely omitted from the text; (b) with having nothing to do with the mother's body and her babies; (c) with enviously arresting the process of daughter's succeeding their mothers and so becoming the new generation of mothers; (d) with enviously substituting the immature daughter for the mature mother; (e) with exerting absolute authority over the female and thus abolishing the contra-polar sexual tension between man and woman; (f) and, in a way, keeping himself at a distance from the primal scene and the danger of the woman, wife and mother, involved in it. This type of paedophilia is not love of the child at all but rather a passion for sabotaging the good primal scene and its consequences in life.

One of the interesting things about this type of negativistic paedophilic perversion is the high degree of unconsciousness with which it is acted out. There is a seeming innocence about it all, as if the person concerned has noticed nothing. It is as if the sixth figure in Meltzer's *dramatis personae* of the primal scene is, despite the description quoted, not seen to be what he is. He is a 'wolf in sheep's clothing', often, indeed, an honoured guest. The author describes his feelings sufficiently artlessly for it to be likely that he has never realized the implications of his secret homosexuality; of his attack on the parents; of his fear of the mother; of his incestuous holding back of his daughter's development into a wife and mother; of his gaining the trust of the young girls' mothers and then betraying it; and of his confusing sadistic excitement with true sensuality. He feels innocent and justified, for he believes that he is a saviour bringing ecstasy into the world. So much does he feel this that he does not wonder why his daughter was unable to make a stable marriage and returned home to him only to become an embittered observer of her father's antics with her successors. He does not notice how premature are the states of sexual excitement that he has induced in the young girls. But it is a dangerous innocence, for he ends up in prison quite unrecognized as a bringer of light and life. The outcome for all concerned is calamitous. Nevertheless, it is impossible not to wonder how deep the 'innocence' really was, for the author does not appear to have taken many precautions against being found out and legally punished. Perhaps, in allowing himself to be apprehended, he was aware at a deeper level of his plight and sought protection for both himself and others from the perverse nature of his acts. This last consideration is as relevant if *Green Fruit* is a fantasy product as if it is a factual account.

Green Fruit represents a crude fantasy of negativistic perverse paedophilic 'acting out', and is at the other end of the spectrum from Paul's fantasies which were more unconscious, subtler and of a more inward nature. Analysts seldom encounter problems of systematically acted out paedophilic perversion in an atmosphere of 'innocence'. They usually deal rather with people whose problems are more piecemeal, often unconscious and subtle. The 'acting out' is often only occasional and then accompanied by guilt and distress.

THE CASES OF CLAUD, ALAN AND JONATHAN

Claud had a lamentable early history of infant neglect, insecurity and trauma and later found the choice of a suitable girlfriend or wife beyond his powers. The early traumas included a series of foreign nurses in the first months of life, absence of his mother, all the subtle disruptions connected with changes of residence, and severe dysentery. He grew up in an extreme love-hate relationship with his mother who, though not young when he was born, was unprepared for motherhood. His father had to go abroad on five-year tours of service interspersed with short visits home to the family. In addition to the damage already done in his parental and familial relationships, an unusual set of calamities in his late teens left him quite alone in the world. Claud's problem was that he had a considerable sexual aversion to mature women. He had relationships with younger women but felt himself attracted to very young, particularly pre-adolescent girls, especially when they had a deceptive air of maturity about them and when they admired him for his mental and artistic qualities. He had considerable pedagogic ability, but there was never any question of actual seduction. His compromise involved being attracted only to women much younger than himself, not necessarily adolescent but generally immature, and the tendency was for each affair, or each marriage, to be disastrous, not so much through neurotic behaviour as through the distinct unsuitability of the young women involved. For a long time, Claud had very little control over these choices which were based upon the hope that the young women would not torment him with the demands made by older women and would not remind him of his mother. The opposite always proved to be the case and the relationships grew to be more

106

and more similar to what he had experienced with his mother. They regularly ended painfully and destructively. Unlike the author of *Green Fruit*, Claud was sophisticated and much less 'innocent'. During the long periods of growing consciousness and analytic 'repair' during treatment, Claud suffered miseries of guilt and frustration from the negative aspects of his paedophilic impulses, though the positive aspects greatly enriched his life.

Another patient, Alan, similarly endowed with positive paedophilic gifts in relation to adolescent boys and girls, but particularly boys, experienced sexual excitement only with a certain type of late adolescent boy. The guilt, alarm and frustration which this caused drove him to seek treatment. His guilt was mainly an expression of uneasiness over a plight that demanded a far higher level of consciousness about his situation than he could muster (guilt feelings can promote consciousness). He was alarmed by the possibility that he might attempt to sexually seduce one of the adolescents because the excitement might become uncontrollable. He might then be overcome with shame whether he were successful or found out or rejected. His pain was further connected with a peculiar frustration. The particular kind of boy that excited him was precisely the kind least likely to respond. These boys were not particularly homosexual, at any rate consciously. They were rather straightforward, athletic and able boys who had girlfriends. Another marked feature of these boys was that their relationships with their mothers was quite satisfactory. They were not bound to them by either extreme fusionary love or hate, but had achieved a reasonable degree of separateness. These were precisely the boys, who, though very fond of Alan no doubt on account of his positive paedophilic capacities, did not wish to enter into reciprocal states of homosexual excitement with him. The fact that they felt threatened in their relationships with their girlfriends probably meant that they sensed deep down that Alan's sexual excitement for them was based upon hatred of the mother, and an envious longing to unite with them and become as they were. Alan's other intense frustration revolved around the question of marriage and children. His deep fear and hatred of women made him unconscious of any sexual attraction towards them and yet he wanted children. If we look into Alan's history we can easily see the pattern of development. The women in his family were dominant, but the males either retiring, bonhomous, or violent. Alan had not had enough experience of being the object of the positive paedophilic impulse. During his adolescence, especially, he felt dominated and fussed over by the women, bullied by a brother and abandoned by his father. This made him feel he had missed his adolescence and so he sought it in the boys he loved. Unlike his father, who was a rationalist, Alan had always held a religious point of view manifested in amiability, youth work and good works in general. Though his family situation had some good aspects and was not wholly destructive, there were violent elements underlying a respectable surface. As I have shown, these manifested themselves in Alan by causing him very great distress and feelings of guilt, alarm and frustration. Psychotherapy greatly eased these tensions and enabled him to live much more constructively and dynamically. He became a fuller person and took on massive responsibility at work. He remained a bachelor, however, but was much more in control of the perverse elements of his paedophilia.

Another patient, Jonathan, exemplifies the gradual emergence of a perverse sadistic paedophilic impulse. Coming from a rather tough, though able, family, his need for love and affection, and to have a 'good enough' experience of the paedophilic impulse in the parental situation, had been inadequately met. How and why was unclear except that constitutionally he started off more sensitive and conscious of his needs than were his siblings. At each point in his life that we discussed, he could remember seeking physical affection and being rebuffed. Little girls, adolescent girls, young women, all seemed to him, at different stages of his life, to retreat from his advances in a way that completely mystified him and increasingly caused in him violent rages. It certainly seemed that he came from stock whose style of life did not include any physical expressions of love and affection. There was no touching of any sort. It appears that the effects of early damage and lack of experience were such that he was ham-fisted in approaching women. His movements tended to be violent and the expression on his face was frightening. His choice of wife rather confirmed his desperation. For she needed a lot of wooing and complained that he had no finesse and lacked understanding of a woman's feelings. Almost certainly he and his wife engendered intense sado-masochistic feelings in each other and her constant rebuttals of his advances led to acts of violence on his part. They seemed locked together in a perverse sexual relationship—frustrating except for verbal and physical violence. Sexual frustration activated a new in-terest in his children. Hitherto, he had focused largely on a lack of discipline in them, allegedly fostered by his wife. Now he began to experience fairly intense incestuous paedophilic feelings towards his adolescent daughters, and to develop a feeling that incest was the most 'natural thing in the world' and society was wrong in condemning it. He found it difficult to understand the significance of the incest taboo or to decide whether sexual relations with his daughters was what he really wanted. Indeed, he could not understand why they, too, should shy away from him apart from their being always under the watchful eye of their mother. The tragedy of Jonathan who was humane, well meaning and amiable in many ways, was that his feeling unloved as a child, his despair about the primal scene and the frenzied impatience of his blundering efforts with women, created an ever increasing sense of emptiness and depression. This drove him to intense perverse, sadistic paedo-philic longings, and into substituting for loving feelings a manic desire for sexual excitement coupled with a background of violence; feelings which he controlled with great difficulty.

THE RELATIONSHIP TO THE THERAPIST

The cases of Claud, Alan and Jonathan illustrate the great

difficulty encountered by the therapist during treatment. Their desperation, in differing degrees, makes them doubt the effectiveness and, in a way, the potency of the therapist. Their envy tends to make them less able to benefit from any interpretations offered to them and makes them ignore any evidence of goodwill or concern on the part of the therapist. Moreover, it is not only envy that causes trouble. In each case, the father was practically a nonentity and failed to relate as a man to the powerful and rather hard mother. The kind of experience these boys had of such a father tends to be repeated with the therapist. Indeed, this is part of the despair which is behind manic perverse paedophilia. It is extremely difficult for people in such a situation to develop an experience of the analyst or therapist as 'good enough'; as a 'good enough' breast or penis, mother or father. Such people find it difficult to feel that they are involved in a 'good enough' primal scene, in whatever form this may take within the therapeutic relationship. They are naturally suspicious of the therapist, as analysis inevitably resembles being with a parent and awakens feelings about the real parents which may have been dormant for years. Furthermore, it is hard for them to feel that analytical interpretations and insights are not really criticism delivered contemptuously. Such patients do not really understand the care and concentrated empathy that lies behind an accurate and telling interpretation of their memories. This means that the analyst will waste his time if his interpretations come only as intellectual propositions. When analysis of such a patient is successful it is because the patient has gradually been able to trust the analyst and has realized that interpretations will have been about the origins of the patient's mistrust of parental figures.

THE NIGHT PORTER

Today analysts and psychotherapists very frequently come across one type of paedophilic problem. Indeed it seems to be one of the great issues in contemporary culture. It can be found in therapy in various forms and disguises, and also in contemporary films and literature. We may consider, as an extreme and grossly concrete example of this, the well-known film *The Night Porter*.

The story illustrates the relationship that exists between the perversion implicit in a political ideology like Nazism, and problems of paedophilic perversion. It is a skilful weaving together of action and psychopathology. In a Nazi concentration camp, a Nazi blackshirt, fully uniformed and jack-booted, is filming by spotlight long lines of naked inmates. The blackshirt, named Max, focuses on a thin young girl and feels a sadistic, paedophilic passion for her. Her response is entirely passive. He films her naked, bullies her, cuts her about and shoots at her naked body with a revolver, aiming to miss. He makes her perform fellatio and other oral sexual acts including nipple sucking at a time when she is half-starved. He has her hair cut short, boy-like, in a homosexual reversal of roles. He makes her watch homosexual buggery taking place in a bed near hers. He dresses her in a child's cotton shift and calls her 'my little girl'. He dresses her in trousers and braces and makes her perform as a bare-breasted singer and dancer in a nightclub full of silent watching Nazis. The film powerfully creates an atmosphere of perversion. There is a silent, sado-masochistic relationship between the Nazi warders and the hungry prisoners. The prisoners are absolutely passive. An almost catlike smile flickers on Max's watchful face. There is a very strong element of voyeurism: the filming, the silent watching of the buggery by the inmates, the silent watching of a male ballet dancer's performance by the S.S. men and the silent watching of the girl's song and dance. One day, Max, having heard that she did not like one of the male prisoners, has his head cut off and presented to her, not on a platter as in the case of John the Baptist but in a cardboard box covered by a rough cloth.

Years later, in postwar Vienna, Max is a night porter. His guilt about the past and fear of present retribution make him hate the light of day. In the hotel where he works there are two permanent residents from the Third Reich: one an elderly countess for whom he procures drugs and hires a young man to warm her when she needs it, though he treats her roughly and contemptuously. And there is a male ballet dancer, previously a Nazi, who dances for him in the middle of the night as he works the spotlight, and to whom he administers drugs. We are clearly shown his homosexual contempt for the mother—the elderly woman—and the homosexual care for the ballet dancer, more tender but still tinged with contempt.

Max and the ballet dancer belong to a small group of ex-Nazis including the medical officer now acting as their group psychiatrist, all of whom had been officers in the original concentration camp. The aim of the group is to rehabilitate themselves so that they can again live their lives as members of society just as they did in the past. The doctor's idea is to 'clean up' each member by getting him to confess to the group everything that he had done in the camp with the hope of easing his guilt. The other, more sinister, aspect was to abolish all documentary evidence of their criminal actions in the camp and to search out all possible eye-witnesses from the past who might give information about them to the police. These people were to be ruthlessly silenced by that kind of extermination that leaves the police little to go on. They had all been cleared except for Max who was half-hearted about the project. He did not find confession to the group helpful. He felt guilty and wished to avoid the light and simply to be left alone to live quietly 'like a church mouse'. He had no desire to become a potent man again, perhaps because he had never been one before. In his case, however, there were two witnesses left. One was Mario, who only wanted a quiet life and ran a successful little restaurant. He promised Max that he would not inform the police but Max had no compunction about eliminating him by pushing him overboard on a fishing expedition, just to be on the safe side. The affair was hushed up and the police practically persuaded that it was an accident. There was one other witness, however, whom Mario recognized from a photograph, and that was Max's 'little girl' from the concentration camp. For Max's fellow ex-Nazis, there was no problem. The witness was to be tracked down and, if there was any suspicion at all, eliminated. Any danger to their group's social rehabilitation was to be ruthlessly removed. Max had other ideas, however, and would not admit to recognizing her.

One evening, a couple book in at the hotel. They are an orchestral conductor and his American wife, beautifully dressed, *soignée* and sophisticated. The conductor, in Vienna to conduct *The Magic Flute*, is portrayed as looking rather like Max, but psychologically potent. His American wife is Max's 'little girl'. There is immediate mutual recognition accompanied by shattering inner disturbance. Unconscious and elemental processes take over. The past is no longer the past, but present and immediate. Without conscious or verbalized planning they meet and her husband, who has been sent off by his wife to complete his European tour alone, is not contacted. Sex is taken up in the same mode as in the concentration camp, beginning with an extra demonstration of manic violence and responsiveness on the part of the 'little girl'. Max expresses a mixture of brutality and maternal tenderness in the loudly excited, mutually responsive, encounter. As before, oral sexuality predominates and, as before, the 'little girl' is almost totally silent and submissive. She then goes to live with Max in his flat and becomes involved again in bloodletting, mutually sado-masochistic sexuality and is kept literally chained in the flat when Max leaves to go to work. Finally, Max abandons his job but will not admit to the members of the ex-Nazi group what is happening in the flat. They, however, know that he has the girl with him. For the group there is only one way to protect their safety: the execution of both Max and the girl. They keep watch continuously on the flat, bribe the grocer not to deliver any food, cut off the electricity and shoot Max in the hand when he goes out on to the balcony. A period of 'imprisonment' in the flat follows, both Max and the girl growing weaker and more emaciated from lack of food while the girl becomes as she had been in the concentration camp. They spend their time on sex and sadism, to the degree that their physical weakness allows it—hungry and without light as it had been in the camp. Then one night, after their sex had been more genital, Max breaks down. He psychotically dresses himself in his blackshirt uniform and boot, takes the girl, who by then looks like an emaciated doll, and drives with her into the night followed by the ruthless ex-Nazi group. Walking across a bridge over the Danube, they are shot in the back and killed instantly.

Thus the past became almost exactly reproduced in the present. The sadistic, perverse paedophilic obsession had in no way changed over the intervening ten years save that the girl was more sexually aggressive, perhaps as a result of her marriage. A kind of tenderness persisted and even developed alongside their insoluble problem. They were impotently caught up in their sado-masochism from which they could no more escape than they could the ex-Nazi group. This tragic ending no doubt had its roots in the psychotic collective upheaval in the German psyche expressed in the noticeably perverse, though covert, accompaniments of Nazism, however much the overall policy made itself out to be opposed to perversion. Nevertheless, Max's personal illness and depressive impotence must have had its roots in his early life. We are given few clues, though he treats the ageing mother figure of the resident countess with roughness and contempt. She is portrayed as being dependent on drugs and young men for her survival. Furthermore, Max's homosexual feelings towards the ballet dancer and his tendency to dispense maternal care, intermixed, however, with angry outbursts, seem to suggest a rejection of the mother as inadequate and an identification with the mother as the only way of securing the presence of a mother at all. The perverse and sadistic paedophilia, and indeed the voyeurism focused upon youthful beauty, can then be seen as a defence against the depression and loneliness of the emotional desert in which he found himself. *The Night Porter* is a film that illustrates well how sure the artist's touch can be in portraying the psycho-dynamics of human beings when they are consumed by the excitement of the many sadistic perversions of the primal scene.

III

PAEDOPHILIA AND THE INNER CHILD

So far we have been dealing with paedophilia mainly in terms
of varying kinds of relationships with real boys or girls. It is
true that Alan's love of straight boys who had good relationships with their mothers was deeply influenced by his own
needs. These boys were an image of his own missing adolescence. It was as if the image of what he had never been
could replace its reality; as if sexual union with the boys
would give him the experience of adolescence he had missed.
His real need was to be in touch with an inner adolescent
freshness in a way appropriate to his age. This is not to deny
that for some older people, closeness to adolescents enlivens,
stimulates and to some degree renews. Actually Alan did
appreciate something of this and as a result grew more open
and spontaneous—no mean achievement for an apparently
conventional man.

The kind of paedophilia, therefore, which we have not
discussed contains a much a greater degree of projection in
it than any so far dealt with. Here a part of a person is first
discovered through its being mirrored by another person. Jung
and Kerenyi[6] have described for us various aspects of the
archetype of the divine child. For them part of this archetype
is connected with the positive image of the hero who succeeds
in surviving and achieving great things, though emerging from
an unfavourable, often orphaned, background with cruel and
inhumane foster-parents. The hero has an almost charmed
life and appears invulnerable, or at least ultimately triumphant, either in this world or the next. Jung painted the image

[6] C. G. Jung and C. Kerenyi, *Introduction to a Source of Mythology:
The Myth of the Divine Child and the Mysteries of Eleusis*, tr.
R. F. C. Hill. London 1951.

mainly in positive terms though there is also a negative aspect to it. Thus Frieda Fordham[7] has described the more negative aspects in terms of the hero's omnipotent envy, contempt and defiance of the parents, who are felt to have betrayed and ill-treated him. As a result, he has to develop a rootless, do-it-yourself psychology. Nevertheless, the divine child or the hero represents a potential in the human psyche. This potential for renewal, recreation and rebirth has much more to do with the future than the past. Its apt image is often a beautiful youth full of promise for the future, gazing out to endless horizons. It is the fate of certain youths to become for older people the symbol of their future, resurrection and rebirth. The image of a potential within the adult is mirrored by an actual youth. Through this, something new may be stimulated in the adult provided that he can withdraw the projection sufficiently, or at least provided that he does not miss the whole point and embark on some outer erotic adventure with the youth. We should, however, add at this point that even in the extreme examples of perverse sadistic paedophilia, something of this ideal subjective element comes in. It is with this latter, in one of its forms in literature, that we shall deal in the next section.

DEATH IN VENICE

A classical account of this kind of experience on a multi-dimensional level is Thomas Mann's *Death in Venice*,[8] a deeply moving piece of exact observation and artistic insight into the inner experience of a great literary artist a few weeks before his death. Here the experience of the divine youth, exemplified by a beautiful boy of about fifteen, is woven into the total fabric of a fulfilled yet profoundly exhausted life so that it becomes a focal point in its unconscious preparation for death.

[7] Frieda Fordham, 'The Case of Regressed Patients and the Child Archetype' *Journal of Analytic Psychology* (1964 Vol. 9 No. 1).
[8] Thomas Mann, *Stories and Episodes*, tr. H. T. Lowe Porter. Everyman 1962.

Aschenbach, the central character, was a literary artist, coming from Silesian stock on his father's side—officers, judges, departmental functionaries—men who lived their strict, decent, sparing lives in the service of King and State. His mother, on the other hand, was the daughter of a Bohemian musical conductor, and the combination of the two streams produced an artist of exquisite sensibility and discipline. He was an early genius, a little delicate and therefore educated at first, at home. Nevertheless, almost before he left school, he had made a name. His literary life was arduous and demanding in the extreme. For him, the anti-hero in his famous book *The Abject* was the object of his furious condemnation. 'Explicitly he renounced sympathy with the abyss and "the flabby humanitarianism" of the phrase "*tout comprendre, c'est tout pardonner*"' (p. 80). Instead, his hero expressed an 'aristocratic self-command that can conceal to the last moment its inner undermining and its biological decline from the eyes of the world' (p. 78). It was 'the conception of an intellectual and virginal manliness, which clenches its teeth and stands in modest defiance of the swords and spears that pierce its side' (p. 75). A life lived like this naturally leaves its mark upon the facial features, but also generates a fatigue and longing for freshness and renewal as the years pass by. One day, walking in Munich, Aschenbach was struck by the sight of a strange, arrogant Austrian carrying a rucksack and stick; he had restless eyes, two pronounced furrows in his forehead, a snub nose and head raised 'so that the Adam's apple looked very bald in the lean neck rising from the loose shirt' (p. 71). Aschenbach found himself becoming suddenly restless for release from strain. He felt the need to go to the warm South and immediately made arrangements to leave for Venice.

On the boat to Venice from Pola he saw another disturbing sight: an elderly man aping the young, dressed in an absurdly juvenile way and grotesquely, even obscenely, besporting himself in the company of a crowd of roistering young clerks out to enjoy themselves on a trip to Venice. The solitary Aschenbach—his greatly loved wife had died young and adored daughter was now grown up and married—found during the first evening in his hotel on the Lido a new and overwhelming vision. There was an aristocratic and beautiful Polish woman, alone with her children and their nurse. The girls in the family were hideously dressed as if to hide whatever incipient beauty they might have begun to possess. But the boy was exquisitely beautiful: his features perfectly formed, his hair golden and curly, simply and beautifully dressed in a sailor-suit, poised in his movements, spontaneous yet gravely dignified and with the faintest smile upon his lips. He appeared to Aschenbach to be divinely formed. For some days the latter spent much time sitting on the beach and gazing at the boy as he artlessly played with young admiring friends for whom he was a kind of aristocrat. He watched him being cossetted and loved by his mother and his nurse. The boy was clearly not unconscious of Aschenbach and on one occasion the faint pre-smile became a direct one for Aschenbach alone. The latter, who had learned that the boy's name was Tadzio, was overwhelmed and disturbed by this smile but was able to rationalize his feelings by ascribing them to the effects on his system of the Sirocco wind, giving him headaches through the combined effects of stimulation and enervation. He was tempted to make a bolt for it before he was lost, and got as far as the railway station. However, circumstances and a half-unconscious wish to see the boy made him return with almost a light heart and a gay smile. His days passed; he watched the boy regularly and with the inspiration of Tadzio's not too distant bodily presence on the beach, Aschenbach was able to write a short but exquisite piece of prose on a topic recently raised by the literateurs of his circle.

Meanwhile, a shadow was settling over Venice and the Lido. The threat of cholera, about which a real conspiracy of silence was being maintained for the sake of the tourist trade, was nevertheless slowly emptying the hotel and the town. The smell of disinfectant pervaded the city, a sign of threatening disease and death. One night a grotesque party of Italian singers sang to the guests on the terrace of the hotel. Aschenbach sat there while Tadzio leant characteristically against the railings six paces away from him and listened too. The strange Austrian that Aschenbach had seen in Munich and who had filled him with restlessness, seemed to have a double in a singing guitarist. The singer had the same furrowed brows, the same snub nose and the same bold Adam's apple showing through his open-necked shirt. He came near to Aschenbach who was able to ask him about the cholera. 'The cholera! What cholera?' replied the singer as he accepted his tip. He then began a song, primitive and wordless, composed of laughing sounds to an infectious tune. False and manic peals of laughter were repeated again and again. The whole hotel was in fits of laughter. Aschenbach watched Tadzio's slightly aloof aristocratic manner. The singer retired. The incident was over. The next day Aschenbach went to an exchange bureau and saw an honest-looking Englishman behind the counter. He ventured to ask him about the cholera. He was taken aside and told the truth. Hundreds had died. The hospitals were full. Venice would soon be blockaded. The cholera had spread from the East. He was advised to leave at once. Aschenbach found himself longing to warn the beautiful mother to take the children—and Tadzio—to safety. He did not, though, for he knew that words with the mother would bring him back to himself—and who, when he is beside himself, wants to be brought back to reality?

Something else was taking place in Aschenbach. He thought it might be fitting to exchange words with the boy after many days of silent, voyeuristic and occasionally reciprocated glances. He prepared to do so the next time the boy passed his way. When the boy finally did appear, however, Aschenbach could not speak—for emotion and breathlessness—and the opportunity was missed. Perhaps Aschenbach did not really want to break the spell by words and wished to continue to surrender himself to the wordless experience. So now he gave himself over to the spell. He became inflamed with passion for the boy. His dreams became chaotic, filled with orgiastic images reminiscent of bacchanalian or dionysian revels. He followed the boy everywhere from afar. Often the boy would drag behind his nurse and sisters to turn and look, only to be chivvied to keep up by the nurse. Aschenbach also surrendered to the blandishments of his Italian hairdresser and permitted him to darken his grey hair, to freshen the skin of his face, and to rouge his lips and cheeks. The result was reminiscent of the image of the elderly man playing the juvenile on the ship from Pola to Venice.

The days went by until, one morning, Aschenbach came down and saw the luggage of Tadzio's family in the hall of the hotel. They were to depart that day. Onto the nearly empty beach Aschenbach moved, haltingly, for he had been feeling very unwell for some days. He slumped in his chair and watched Tadzio. A quarrel arose between Tadzio and his simpler, coarser boy companion, Jaschiu. The latter was angry at Tadzio for throwing sand at him and challenged him to a fight. The coarser boy overcame the more refined and weaker one. Jaschiu pinned the exhausted boy face downwards on the sand, humiliated. Aschenbach tried to move to rescue Tadzio. It was not necessary; Jaschiu let him go. Tadzio was angry. He shrugged off Jaschiu who now felt sorry and wanted to make it up. Tadzio broke away, ran to the water's edge and waded in until he reached the sandbar, then began to move leftward, where he paused, his face turned seaward. He paced about in moody pride. Then

once more he paused to look: with a sudden recollection, or by an impulse, he turned from the waist up, in an exquisite movement, one hand resting on his hip, and looked over his shoulder at the shore. The watcher sat just as he had sat that time in the lobby of the hotel when first the twilit grey eyes had met his own. He rested his head against the chair-back and followed the movements of the figure out there, then lifted it, as it were in answer to Tadzio's gaze. It sank on his breast, the eyes looked out beneath their lids, while his whole face took on the relaxed and brooding expression of deep slumber. It seemed to him the pale and lovely Summoner out there smiled and beckoned; as though with the hand he lifted from his hip, he pointed outward as he hovered on before into an immensity of richest expectation.

Some minutes passed before anyone hastened to the aid of the elderly man sitting there collapsed in his chair. They bore him to his room. And before nightfall a shocked and respectful world received the news of his decease. (p. 152)

THE PAEDOPHILIC IMPULSE AND REBIRTH

This famous ending of *Death in Venice* eloquently describes the deepest meaning of the paedophilic impulse when we focus upon it as an expression of the inner life of the adult. Tadzio, who never speaks, is a highly suitable projection screen upon which to glimpse the image of the divine child, the *puer aeternus*, the renewing and resurrecting spirit in the ageing Aschenbach, almost his anticipated reborn spirit as he prepares for death and indeed meets it. Thomas Mann intensifies the projection screen aspect of Tadzio for Aschenbach by permitting no knowledge, no information and no verbal self-explanation to pass from one to the other. Aschenbach gazed and interpreted what he saw. Involuntarily, memories of his past must have been awakened, for what he saw was something similar to the picture of the young Aschenbach as painted by Mann: the young Aschenbach was slight and constitutionally rather frail. He was recognized as gifted and as a result educated at home with his mother. He was indeed special. And that is what Aschenbach interpreted as he watched how the women handled Tadzio. Again, for Aschenbach's literary ideals and achievements, the perfect marriage of form and content in an exquisite sensibility was always the aim. He saw in Tadzio a matching of beauty with a spontaneity of movement allied to a just perceptible aloofness expressing an aristocratic sense of responsibility born out of good breeding. These qualities, physically expressed by

Tadzio, were almost exactly the image of Aschenbach's quality of writing. Again, the grave and steady gaze of Tadzio represented a youthful version of a similar quality of facial expression that had developed over the years in Aschenbach. Apart from this, how strikingly apt for the ageing Aschenbach were the adjectives 'grey' and 'twilit' which he applied to the eyes of Tadzio. Above all, perhaps, the final striking posture of the boy gazing out to sea into 'an immensity of richest expectation' represented a profound image of the quality and direction of Aschenbach's literary work.

There was, however, something different in the boy for all that. Apart from the fineness of feeling, the marked feature was his physical constitution and look. It was exuberant and fresh. In a way, it was something that Aschenbach had always missed. His artistic genius and his particular ideals specialized him in certain directions at the expense of his physical constitution. Indeed it had worn him out and he was tired at a very deep level. However, Thomas Mann makes him eager to live to a good age. He is not satisfied with the ardently lived first fifty or so years of his life. He is, anyway, bereft of a loved wife through her death, and of his daughter through marriage. But he has had no son onto whom he can project the image of renewal, or through whom he can fulfil himself in parenthood. Something of his unlived physical existence is beginning to press upon him. It makes its first insistence through the striking image of the physical, snub-nosed, outdoor Austrian traveller with his Adam's apple freely bared through his open-necked shirt. The image of the Adam's apple has, no doubt, a rich history in itself, but the male sexual freedom that Mann's image symbolizes is striking in its concreteness. It stimulates something that is ready to emerge in a very positive form: a desire to be renewed, to be enhanced by a physically based experience, by travel to a new place; a journey to the South. There is an insolence about the man, quite unimpressed by the presence of a great literary artist. It is a demand from another and unlived side of Aschenbach's nature.

And yet, the appeal has something primitive, crude, undifferentiated, even false about it. Indeed, it is surely a sign of Mann's artistic clarity of insight that he shows it to be so. There is a streak in Aschenbach which is not entirely integrated and hence false: the possibility of aping the young can express itself in the grotesque image of the elderly man of Pola on the ship to Venice. Once this falseness is mirrored, however, his integrity permits him to see the absurdity of the notion that the freshness of unlived early life could be secured by antics such as these. It represents a possibility though it is rejected in horror. And yet, when near madness descends upon Aschenbach, he surrenders to the attempts of his hairdresser to plaster onto the external appearance of an older man the unconvincing and artificial looks of youth. It is an inferior all-too-human shadow aspect of Aschenbach as he struggles with his problem of unlived life. This shadow impulse also surfaces through another very striking image— that of the crude Italian guitar player and singer. He is boldly extrovert and makes a living in a crude way. He, too, like the Austrian stranger displays the naked Adam's apple through his loose shirt. He also generates manic laughter through his 'ha-ha' song without words. He, too, uses the technique of a false laughing defence at a time when decay and death are in the air. Venice is in the grip of cholera. Aschenbach is old and almost dying. And, six paces away, representing something real and palpable and no false imitation of youth, stands Tadzio. The dramatic contrast is almost unbearable. Yet, for the moment, the turmoil in Aschenbach is such that he surrenders to the banal and insensitive song of the guitarist —no criticism here—for vulgarity is not entirely inappropriate at times in the dynamism of an exquisite like Aschenbach.

For one as spiritual as Aschenbach, the compensatory processes of the psyche can manifest themselves in concrete images such as the deeply disturbing and shattering dreams that overwhelmed him during the period of his madly obsessive love for Tadzio. The dreams, familiar enough to analysts for some decades—though in this case the product of a creative artist like Thomas Mann writing in 1910—contained a tremendous outburst of orgiastic fantasies. These are obviously compensatory in an artist as patently disciplined, intellectual and full of sensibility as Aschenbach. For anyone, and particularly Mann, steeped as he was in classical learning, the image takes on the form of bacchanalian and dionysian revels and orgies vividly dramatized, as, for instance, in the plays of Aristophanes.

For analysts today, the experience would, no doubt, illustrate the way in which excluded life impulses return and insist upon recognition in some form or other. Aschenbach was not exempt from this basically human process. We may understand, furthermore, how images like that of the Austrian stranger, assailing him at a time of deadly fatigue, were so basically physical. Similarly, it is understandable how naturally the deep paedophilic impulse towards Tadzio falls into a central place within a plethora of images related to decline, death and rebirth. The fate of Tadzio, the actual boy, in that particular year of his life was that he would be, for a few weeks, a mirror, a projection screen for a great artist at a point in the latter's life where ambiguity about the future prevailed. Was it that Aschenbach would be living a renewed life, right into his eighties perhaps, as he so strongly, at least consciously, desired? Or was he fated to be on the brink of experiencing the real death of the body, partly in a spirit of revolt against old age and partly imaging the intimations of immortality? It turns out, in Mann's creation, that Tadzio was to become a symbol of the reborn Aschenbach in the latter sense, as he gazed with his grey twilit eyes towards the sea, the original Mother, 'pointing outward, as he hovered on before, into an immensity of richest expectation' (p. 152).

IV

PAEDOPHOBIA

There was a point in *Death in Venice* when Aschenbach became afraid. He feared the shattering effects of Tadzio's smile. His fear drove him to cancel his stay at the Lido, to pack his bags and to run for his life. Chance alone fortified his desire to stay. Though the subject of paedophobia demands greater study than is possible here, we are bound to give it some consideration. Aschenbach acted as if he thought the boy would destroy him in some way; he would be the death of him. On simpler, more banal levels, analysts still encounter patients whose mother used a style of expression quite common forty, fifty or sixty years ago: in order to frighten a child into conformity, they would say, 'You'll be the death of me'. Thus in both mother and child, a malign *folie à deux* would develop, whereby the mother confused the real child with the inner image of the heroic, formidable and invulnerable divine child, while the child's belief in, and fear of, his omnipotence would be supported and reinforced by his mother's feelings and words. Today, we can see the anxiety and fear aroused by such a conviction in a child. His grasp of the difference between his inner world of fantasy and belief and the outer world of fact remains weak and unsure, and unconsciously he can become guiltily 'convinced' of his lethal potential.

Patients, sometimes, have only to hear themselves speak aloud to realize how absurd their half-consciously held positions are. For instance, Daniel, who, before he was a year old had been practically orphaned and in fact institutionalized, later married a wife and was very demanding of her love, sympathy and understanding. He would get into violent rages if she ever withheld emotional support of this sort. The question of having a child arose and immediately he heard himself expressing the deepest horror over how the baby, and later the child, would ruin his life, his interests, his circle of friends. It needed only a little effort and help, however, for him to realize the incongruity of his outburst, so that he could consider how he had managed to turn the baby in his fantasy into such a monster. Onto the child was being projected the violent, murderous feelings that he himself had had as an infant and toddler through feeling neglected and prematurely institutionalized. This child within him would at times break out terrifyingly against women, and it was this violence, which was really his own, that was being ascribed to the anticipated real baby. Interestingly enough, as Daniel assimilated this interpretative understanding within his relationship to his analyst whom he saw was not frightened or destroyed by his violence, his tensions and fears eased and he became, over the ensuing years, a devoted and skilled father in whom the paedophobia turned into a positive impulse of paedophilia.

I think that this kind of paedophobia is common and sometimes appears to have a plausible basis. Actually, however, adult paedophobia almost certainly breeds insecurity and, in consequence, violence in the very children that are feared. It is this end product that provides a false feeling of objective justification as if the paedophobia were a response to something more objective and real than it really is. It should, perhaps, be added, though it cannot be expanded here, that some of the more horrific examples of child cruelty and baby-battering have their roots in paedophobia. A delusion develops in the adult that the demands of a deeply disturbed infant or young child are of such intensity as to raise the issue of survival: who will survive—the adult or the child? For the enraged and terrified adult it has become a question no longer of both/and but rather of either/or.

V
PAEDOPHILIA IN PERSPECTIVE

The paedophilic impulse is present in some form or other in all adults although its status in the emotional life and activity of any particular individual is largely determined by his youthful experiences of the paedophilic attitudes displayed towards him by adults in his family, school, youth clubs etc. The individual tends either to exhibit the main features of his childhood experiences or to go into reaction against them, unless he experiences a therapeutic intervention. A fundamental distinction needs to be drawn between creative and destructive elements in paedophilia. Furthermore, when it is directed outwards towards real children in the parental or educational function it appears to be largely different from the paedophilia which represents a projection upon real children or young people of the image of the *puer aeternus*—the divine child of renewal and resurrection and a figure of the inner world of the psyche.

The age-old phenomenon of paedophilia may be understood as an environmental ingredient that is fundamental to the growth processes of children, even, to some extent, in its less benign seeming forms. However, if imperfections in the 'primal scene' become too great, then critical and cynical aspects of it in the child's mind begin to develop as a substitute: fantasies of sexually perverse, sadistic deviations. Perverse paedophilic adults may lead the young thus prepared into premature sexual experiences of this sort in an over-enthusiastic attack upon the 'primal scene' and family life which have been experienced as 'not good enough'.

The case of Paul illustrates an admixture of feeling often found in everyday life. By contrast, the perverse behaviour described in *Green Fruit* illustrates a full-blown calamitous and destructive expression of paedophilia that leads to disaster all round. The cases of Claud, Alan and Jonathan demonstrate variants of paedophilic desire, with the first two able to make good progress under treatment. *The Night Porter* illustrates perverse sadistic paedophilia with despair and death as the final goal of two profoundly disturbed individuals caught up in the collective psychosis of Nazism.

By contrast, the classic literary expression of paedophilia originating from the inner world of a great artist exhausted, ill and ageing, is provided in Thomas Mann's *Death in Venice*. Aschenbach projects the image of the divine child of resurrection and renewal upon the beautiful youth Tadzio and, in the event, dies with the vision before his eyes.

This archetypal image, however, sometimes leads people into experiences of paedophobia. Aschenbach feared the profound change suggested by the figure of Tadzio. Daniel, on the other hand, anticipated with fear that his forthcoming baby would ruin his whole life, while the parents of battered babies seem to fear that the cries and screams of their inconsolable babies will destroy their peace of mind. In fact, it appears in these two instances that the real and highly vulnerable babies have been confused with internal images of the divine child or hero fantasized as monstrously strong.

4

A Struggle for Normality

Mary Williams

In the previous chapters the writers have described normal and abnormal paedophilia and have shown how early childhood and the prevailing culture influence the boundaries between these categories as in the related problems of heterosexuality and homosexuality.

A paedophilic's struggle towards normality through marriage, and its effects on his wife and children is the theme of this chapter. This struggle is seen through the treatment of a couple who were mainly seen together.

As Michael and Erna came into my room, I had a fleeting impression of a fair and willowy youth with a rosebud mouth, and a desperately plain and gawky schoolgirl. In fact, Michael at twenty-eight was tall and substantially built, and I noticed his strong wrists and ankles with a slight sense of shock. The youth's fair and curling locks were now darkened and discreetly cut, and his dress formal. Formally, too, he held the door for his wife and stood until she was seated.

Erna chose a chair near to me. She did not look at either of us. While Michael filled his chair and sat back in a relaxed manner, she was tense, her small body perched on the edge, her head bent, dark hair falling over her face. Her skin, where visible, was mottled as if with continual crying.

They came on the advice of a social worker at the hospital where Erna had had both her children, a girl now four and a boy of two. The boy was a Rhesus baby born by Caesarian section and required a blood exchange. The mother developed complications, thus proving that her catastrophic feelings about maternity were correct. These feelings existed since her first pregnancy, which was uneventful, and accounted for numerous symptoms from migraines to abdominal pains, for which no physical cause could be found.

Erna was suffering greatly from her husband's infidelity and from his unannounced absences, for she particularly dreaded being left alone. This dread echoed and re-echoed childhood experiences in Germany during the war, first through the loss of her father, who was reported missing but whose death was not established for some years, and then in flight before the oncoming Russian armies, often cold, starving and terrified. Erna, unlike her elder sister, did not take comfort from the presence of her mother, for she was too young not to believe that her mother was implicated in her sufferings.

Erna grew up alienated from her mother and escaped as soon as she could as an *au pair* in other countries. Everywhere she suffered from mysterious feelings of depression rather than the feeling of relief and freedom which she had hoped for. She met Michael while working in university lodgings in England and was grateful when he took an interest in her. He was the only boy who had. He encouraged her to confide in him and he told her a good deal about himself.

Michael was then twenty-two and had been seeing a psychiatrist intermittently for over two years. He had been referred by a medical social worker to whom his mother had confided during her hospital examinations for migraine, asthma and associated disorders, and to whom she turned again when her son was caught interfering with small boys at a school where he was filling in time before taking up a university scholarship. Her reaction was to threaten to kill herself if he ever did such a thing again. She also cried dreadfully when he announced his forthcoming marriage and could not bring herself to go to the ceremony; neither could his father. Michael felt their disappointment in him deeply, but was helpless to put anything right, or to repay them for all the sacrifices

130

they had made to give him a good start. Michael was their only living child. A stillborn baby with multiple abnormalities who followed him had had to be dismembered in order to complete the birth. His mother told him this and other gruesome stories about her health and sex life while he was still a young child and repeated them often with tears of self-pity. His father had more or less opted out, retiring into his study, so that the two of them were often together. Not only was Michael his mother's confidant, but was also her nurse, having been taught to massage her head, stroke her back, or whatever part of her body she felt needed attention. She seemed oblivious of the seductive nature of her demands and it is probable that she imagined the roles to be reversed and that she was the child of her son, and therefore innocent of seeking erotic gratification. A strong physical resemblance between mother and son made such role swapping easier. Both were fair and blue-eyed.

Michael's remembered reactions to his mother's demands involved feelings of revulsion accompanied by a compulsive attentiveness. This masked his attraction to his mother's body as well as the degree of his resentment about the bonds she imposed, which kept him from meeting his contemporaries. When he was older his longing for freedom led to 'escapes'. He went on foraging expeditions in the nearby town seeking fair, blue-eyed boys resembling himself whom he would induce to touch his penis. In such activities his position as the boy lover of the mother was reversed and he became, as it were, the seductive mother to those little boys, who were mirror images of his young self. This gave him the assurance that he had a penis. An alternative to these fleeting affairs with boys was to seek normality through women. He felt drawn to fair, blue-eyed girls whom he beguiled with a show of interest in much the same way as he did with the boys. He could enjoy them sexually only if they made no demands on him so that those who longed for a deeper relationship were deserted. A different sort of woman were those who were unlike his mother. They were small, dark girls of academic bent who appealed to his

131

intellectual interests. He felt less threatened by these girls, but the sexual interest was not strong and quickly died.

Michael was not without feelings of dismay for what so many people assured him was heartless sensation seeking, but his critical self was a detached observer with no influence over his behaviour. He feared he would come to a bad end and had horrible fantasies of man's corruption, both of his soul and body. He dreaded reaching the age of thirty, which would soon be upon him, and regarded it as the beginning of the end.

His intellectual life was no compensation. Years of effort writing novels had foundered on his inability to imagine the predicaments of those different from himself and he lived on the edge of the literary world in a publisher's office, sub-editing technical books in which he had no interest. Erna would have enjoyed his job, for she had a precise and tidy mind and a good eye for detail. Sometimes she prevailed on him to bring some work home for her to do. She hoped it would also ensure his presence at home but he was just as likely to resent this attempt to trap him and go to visit a girlfriend.

After some unease at the beginning of the first interview,[1] Erna complained that there was no communication between them as all trust had been lost. Discussion of all issues whether practical or emotional was avoided though this did not prevent sudden flare-ups. These were dreadful and resolved nothing as they usually ended with Michael rushing out of the house, the children being upset, and her life being that much harder to cope with. Life was hard enough, she complained, having to look after lodgers to make ends meet, without having to worry whether Michael was going to come back or not.

Her bitterness flowed over him in a steady stream and he started to move about uneasily and once glanced at the door. When she stopped talking Michael felt he had to start. First he defended himself by pleading immaturity; his psychiatrist had told him he was too immature to marry. He knew he was

---

[1] First interviews with couples can be revealing if the therapist aims to facilitate communication between the couple and avoids interventions, other than those necessary for the sake of clarity.

difficult to be married to, but he was very fond of Erna and did not like seeing her unhappy. His feeling was that she expected him to conform to the pattern of a husband that she had in her mind. He felt that he was being asked to deny his own nature. He repeated that he would like to make Erna happy, but he never got an answer to what she wanted of him. He would do anything, except what was contrary to his own nature.

Erna answered him as I felt she had many times before. She wanted him *there* to give her some support. She said that he knew she was frightened of being alone and was overburdened. She had tried to tolerate his mistresses and to overlook his unfaithfulness. She had even gone away, but whatever she did made no difference. Turning to him she said: 'You'll do exactly what you want regardless of how your dependents feel.' Michael replied to her directly saying that he felt her going away had made a difference. Erna had gone to her continental home and he had followed her. He had not been happy in a country in which he could not understand much of the conversation, but he liked her people. In England, the situation was reversed. Erna was the stranger and she had no one but him to fall back on. When they had moved into their present house, she retreated into her previous position. Erna said that she had enjoyed the social whirl in her own town as it was an escape, but it felt unreal as no one knew the truth about their marriage. After a silence, Michael said that in a curious way the non-relationship they had was closer than a more social one. 'The feelers go out from a deep animal level.' Erna didn't feel that at all, the very idea made her shudder. Erna then complained that they had nothing to share. Michael had his own friends and interests already. She had to seek her own. His failure to enjoy the children or to visualize their needs worried her. For instance, he had absented himself when one of the children was ill. And he made her feel guilty when she had a migraine. She tried to say nothing as she knew he would either go out or stay in the office. Michael was staggered at this picture of himself, particularly about the child's illness. He hadn't realized the situation until she rang the office at 8.30 p.m. She reminded him that he did not come home until 1.0 a.m. They stared at each other uncomprehendingly.

I remarked on their different methods of dealing with anxiety. She made appeals through illness, her own or the children's, while he removed himself, escaping from it and even forgetting the cause. There was no need to elaborate further. Michael saw the connection with his past relationship with his mother and more besides. He remembered how often he had seen his mother throwing migraines at his father and himself! His father retired to work and he was left with his mother until he also learnt to escape. He started to speak faster, first about his mother and then about his wife. How his mother had changed from the early days when he remembered her as attempting total self-denial to seeking total self-gratification. She used to avoid company in case something was asked of her; it was a great fear. Then she demanded the best of everything. Then Michael switched the conversation to his wife's second pregnancy. It was a bad time for him. She had a Caesarian section because she was Rhesus negative, her kidneys were affected, she was bleeding copiously, and the child had to have a blood exchange. Michael found it horrifying. And then her wound would not heal and she was at home in bed. He had to be mother to the first child. It lasted only a week but it seemed to him like a year. He had a relationship with another woman too and she was pestering him. His reserves were exhausted. He felt so threatened by the sick wife and the tiny shrivelled child that he went away.

The similarity of Michael's horror reaction to his mother's description of the stillborn infant struck me, as did the transformation of his wife into his mother. But Erna hardly heard him, so deep was her resentment. Michael left the same day as her mother who had come to England and stayed for two weeks after the birth. He had said he was sick of having a mother figure round his neck and vowed that he would go away for an unspecified period as soon as her mother left—

134

whether for three days, three weeks or three months he didn't say. Erna had to rely on neighbours to come in as she was still in bed. Michael also turned against his daughter who had convulsions when he left.

At this point Erna started to cry. Inconsequentially, she apologized to her husband saying, 'Sorry, you go on.' Michael admitted that he developed an antipathy to the boy. He could hardly bear to look at him, and hated being left alone with him. But he had felt differently since the boy had become strong and healthy looking. He had never turned against his daughter, nor had he ever wished his son ill. Erna pursued him with instances of his cruelty towards the boy and her need to protect him. At first he denied everything but then admitted he *had* sometimes hit the boy and felt resentment against him early on. But he denied that he had just deserted her as she claimed. A colleague had promised to help Erna and he didn't know that this colleague was neurotic and hated men and had poisoned Erna's thinking about him. Erna retorted that he had no grounds to complain as she guessed that he had gone to another woman. This he denied. He could not bear the thought of any more demands on him. And he had gone back to her after three days.

He could not imagine Erna's agony: three days—it might have been three weeks or three months, or never! He was sunk in his own family pattern from which he needed to escape, while she was sunk in hers. His abrupt disappearances and the uncertainty of his return touched the tragedy of her young life with the disappearance of her father and the uncertainty as to whether he was alive or dead. I noted that in appearance Erna was totally unlike Michael's mother so that his choice in this obvious respect was a contrast to the problematic image of the mother and a means of escaping it. Appearances were indeed deceptive. He had not reckoned on the power of the unconscious choice, which in this case was based much more on psychic factors, on the feeling tone of the person and on the subtle emanation of attitudes.

No word had yet been spoken about problems of sexual

intimacy and it was unclear how the marriage had come about. All I knew was that his psychiatrist thought it was much too early and had interviewed Erna only to meet a stone wall.

Another diagnostic interview was arranged before deciding how best to help. A report that they left the building hand in hand seemed to be a hopeful sign.

At the next visit, Michael was indeed more hopeful, but had hard work extracting any response from his wife. They realized after the first interview that they had avoided discussing the sexual side of the marriage and were anxious to do so. She had a migraine, he said, and he had an attack of irresponsibility. He had buried himself in the British Museum and got lost in a search for some information. Erna had rung up the Superintendent who had dug him out. She wanted him because he had some roofing material in the car and it was raining. He had absented himself the next night and stayed with some people who, Erna thought, didn't even know he was married. She had felt depressed and upset because real communication was impossible, and it seemed he was just about to pack his bags. He denied this. His impression was that the interview had been such a strain that Erna didn't want to come again.

I remarked that he appeared to be seeing all the hopelessness and depression in his wife. He then admitted to his own hopeless feelings at ever being able to fit into his wife's picture of married life. It just wasn't him. It made him feel old and tired (though he was only twenty-eight!). And Erna was always saying such things as: 'Why do you stay? There's nothing in our marriage.' He'd felt that she would be glad to be rid of him. He was just a tribulation to her. His doctor had said that if marriage was such a prison he should leave and find out what it was like to be alone. I said that it was possible he was also afraid of being alone and that perhaps that was why they had come together in the first place.

Erna remained silent so Michael spoke again for both of them. He said he met her in his third year at university. Erna was an *au pair* in his digs. She was the first girl he ever slept with and he was impotent at first and very aware of his inexperience. So much so that when Erna took his penis between her thighs for safety reasons, he thought that was the real thing. It was uncomfortable. The homosexual question came up again and he told her he couldn't love anybody. Erna went back home leaving him confused. She wrote him affectionate, cheering letters and he wrote hysterical, depressive ones.

Michael's finals were 'disastrous' and he took a bad second. He was impelled to run to Erna's home to seek comfort from her and he taught English there until she was ready to return to England. He found it awful arriving in England again with no university to go to. And the immigration office gave Erna only a visitor's visa. She got work and her employers tried to obtain a work permit, but without avail. Then Erna joined in the conversation. She said it was a case of marrying or going back home. Michael's psychiatrist wasn't keen on him marrying yet but they had decided to. They got on so well and could talk about everything together. Michael agreed. He had told her all about his sessions too and when his treatment stopped he felt fine. He attributed his cure to Erna. His desire for boys vanished though he slept with other women and told Erna about it just as though she were his doctor. He didn't realize how it might affect her. He relied on her judgement of people. He had learnt how to behave through her. It still puzzled him why she had married him.

Erna explained herself with some animation, addressing me as he had done. She was the black sheep of a conventional family because of her leftish views. She longed to speak the truth as she saw it, but it was not possible in her family. Michael had attracted her in the first place because he was so well-read and broad-minded and interested in the arts. They visited galleries and the theatre together and discussed for hours what they had seen. He was also affectionate, kind and optimistic.

I recalled that Michael had described Erna in the same words when referring to her letters. It appeared that they used to comfort each other like the Babes in the Wood. This was

137

all right while the Wicked Uncles were outside the twosome but now they had got inside and they couldn't help persecuting each other.

Erna continued the story. The first serious crack in their relationship was a pregnancy while Michael was still a student. He presumed she would have an abortion and was cruel when she cried. Previously she had been able to tolerate his girl-chasing exploits as naughty pranks, but after the abortion, when he told her of another woman he had fallen for, she felt dreadful. She realized she had believed that she should do everything to shelter him from his neurosis and to encourage his heterosexuality.

Michael looked at her in amazement. He had felt that he was being smothered by matrimony and had been less and less inclined to go home. On realizing his feelings he arranged with her that he could be out one evening a week, and felt better. However, he never told her which evening he would be out and she would be waiting for him with a meal, her resentment and fear growing. Eventually, he was staying away almost every other night. A friend had told her that Michael thought she had the telephone tapped. It was a facetious remark but she pressed him and he admitted that he *did* think that she checked up on him all the time.

I remarked on the way he put his conscience into his wife and then had to escape from it, as he had had to escape from his mother's expectations of constant attention.

Michael took the limelight off himself and turned it on his wife. He thought the disappearance of her father when she was two was important. Her father was anti-Hitler and was sent with an ambulance unit of dissidents to the most dangerous places. None returned, but they were not presumed dead until 1947. Erna took this to mean that she had no picture of marriage and she agreed that marriage was something she knew only from fairy stories. She then remarked on his mother's jealousy of her when she had their first child. His mother had felt then that she had lost her son, though she was still trying to get him back. One day his mother announced

138

dramatically that she had always feared the Germans would take her lovely boy and they had. Such scenes made Erna feel quite ill, especially as it was not possible to count on her for any help with the children. She had said as much, instancing the loss of her second child. Michael shuddered at this point saying that she had told him that it had had to be dismembered to remove it from her body. His mother had wanted a large family and it was hard being the only one. Erna said it was hard having two children when she was left alone so much and was without any help. She felt trapped at home and was jealous of Michael meeting so many interesting people whom he never brought home.

It seemed to me that his fears were those of getting stuck inside his mother-wife and risking dismemberment, hence his tip-and-run behaviour, and her fears were that he would disappear like her father, be exposed to danger and die. Thus she insisted on knowing where he was and on his coming home, and he resisted because this threatened him.

Erna responded by saying that Michael wanted to see me on his own account about his sexual problems. He said he didn't feel strongly about it now, and asked if she did. Her reply was indirect. She was frightened of the questions the children would ask about their relationship. She felt the same about her visits to the hospital and never knew what to say. She could only make vague statements like 'there's something wrong with my tummy'. She was worried because her daughter had sensed her depression and had a fantasy of an impending separation.

I wondered how strong her family pattern was. The second child was now the same age as she had been when she last saw her father. Did it make separation seem inevitable to her? She looked startled and Michael talked of *his* father who opted out of the family, but never actually left; he just sat silently indoors and went for long walks alone. Michael then tested Erna by remarking that he would have to go North for his firm several times a year. Dismayed, Erna turned to me. 'Have things gone too far?' she asked.

It was clear that her fears created for Michael a dreadful resemblance to his devouring mother. She could not believe this any more than he could believe in her fears of losing contact with him. Yet she was the one most afraid of therapy, and had already 'flown' from the marriage and become quite frigid, while he was now potent but, alas, no longer loving. Maybe both were on the wing with anger and disillusionment while still needing each other: she in order not to be alone and he ... ? Did she no longer fulfil his need to be sheltered from his passion for boys? And how much did he still need to resist being attracted to his own son?

Michael wanted to see me alone for many reasons: to be my special patient, as he had been special to his mother, and to get help with his assessment of his girlfriends, whose apparent irrationalities appalled him. He did not want to discuss the things which really mattered: his relationship with his wife and children and his propensity for boys, because he still hoped to find a woman who would satisfy him. On the other hand, Erna was very reluctant to come except with him. She would sometimes encourage him to come alone as he wished to do, having planted the whole of their troubles on his shoulders, a burden he accepted intellectually but found unbearable emotionally, hence his flights from home.

When Michael came alone his search for a strong passion, a 'suitable' girl, was the major subject of discussion. Erna was no longer an adequate barrier against his passion for boys. Yet the passion-rousing girls were still young prototypes of his mother though he could find little else in their favour. They were 'stupid', and were easily 'conned' by his show of interest and concern. His critical mind watched with detachment and sneered at himself and the girls. However, he could spend hours talking with the other kinds of women who were intelligent, small and dark, like his wife. The split image was made up of several ingredients: mind or intellect versus body or instinctual desire; the exciting, incestuous mother image and the stimulating companion. Trouble occurred whenever the split threatened to close and he had to run to prevent the

140

companion-wife image joining with the exciting and forbidden mother which lay in the background of the devouring one. It was when his wife felt to him like the devourer that he had to escape.

His longing for boys surfaced when neither type of woman welcomed him. Then he was threatened by the fear of appalling loneliness and was liable to feel like an abused child rather than a seductive adult appearing to control the situation as had his mother with him. The attractive boys had always been like his young self—blue-eyed and blond—and his encounters started in much the same way as those with his blonde girlfriends. First, the 'chatting-up' phase in which he made a show of interest and concern with their affairs. Then, once he had won them over, he would persuade them to touch his genitals and to 'massage' his penis, as his mother had induced him to massage her body.

He did not have any interest in the other type of boy, small, dark and intelligent, until the advent of his own son. The girl child, blonde like himself, served to reflect a picture of himself as a loving person and boosted his self-esteem, particularly as she went on adoring him in spite of the pain she felt when he went away. The incident when she was said to have had convulsions after a more than usually dramatic departure, had had the opposite effect on Michael to that which Erna intended. He felt blackmailed and could not help disliking the person who had caused this feeling. As with his blonde mother-women, demands drove him away, especially those based on a cry such as, 'Look what you've done to me.' They reinforced the ever-ready critical observer self who pointed out his lack of feeling and his ruthlessness.

The hopes raised by the preliminary interviews started to fade. Michael's hope that Erna would accept him as he was died an angry and lingering death in her anguished tears and reproaches for his compulsive womanizing. Because of her own pain she was incapable of realizing what she was pushing him towards; of realizing that his anger covered his anguish at being forbidden the alternative to the even more forbidden pursuit of young boys. As for Erna, she tried to endure her anxiety about being left but without success. Taut in every muscle, she tried to avoid voicing the appeals and reproaches which drove him away. Quite soon, a reversal took place. Unable to influence her husband's behaviour, she grew determined to get rid of the cause of her sufferings. One day, in a joint session, she announced, trembling, that she could not live with the anxiety any longer and had consulted a solicitor about a divorce. She would have to plead adultery and name his current girlfriend. Michael behaved like a cornered animal. He crouched and froze, his lips curling to show his teeth. I was not surprised that Erna had been afraid to tell him when she was alone with him. His rational self had been entirely stripped away. Her announcement seemed to make his predicament real—too real to be endured. Erna had been a shield against all those women who would want to grab him, though they in turn were shields against the boys. Becoming coherent at last, he protested that he had broken with his latest girl because she was too pressing but now *she* would have a stick to beat him with. His anger changed to anguish and reproach—exactly the behaviour he so disliked in his wife. But Erna was adamant about her suffering and need for revenge.

This reversal of the positions between the partners marked a stage in which each discovered what it was like to be the other. Neither could then easily escape the knowledge of the ruthlessness of their survival anxiety and the way in which each had been trying to force the other to change in order to avoid facing their own problems.

Erna faced her problem by sticking to her insistence on a divorce in spite of her fear of being alone. Michael found it much more difficult to face his and used every means to shake his wife's resolve. At first he tried to prove by logical argument that separate living was financially impossible and that she would never manage the house without him, and so on. The less successful his arguments, the more irrational he became, until he finally threatened to disappear, a threat

142

calculated to make the maximum impact on her susceptibilities. Erna broke down and cried and he made a clumsy effort to comfort her, so clumsy that he made it easy for her to repulse him.

It was at this point that Michael agreed to take a room away from the house to cool off. They agreed to meet each other by mutual consent while waiting for the divorce, and when they came to sessions with me. It was not until then that Michael's father came into the picture. It seemed he had always been present in a ghostly way as he acted as financial adviser by telephone, and he even held money for his son. Michael's childlike dependence on his father was a revelation to Erna. He had kept his relationship secret in case his mother discovered it and Erna had been put in the same category because he feared she would attempt to destroy it in a jealous rage.

His father had made up for his apparent early indifference to Michael. After he left home they had become very close, confiding to each other over the telephone. Michael had absolute trust in his father's goodwill besides enjoying the clandestine nature of the arrangement. There was probably a homosexual bond between them which, in the absence of contact, was safe from disturbing effects. His father had no objections to the break-up of his marriage and even helped to smooth the way, whereas his mother wrote furious letters to Erna for daring to threaten to expose her son in open court as an adulterer, and made counter-accusations. Again, Erna was amazed as she believed that her mother-in-law would be glad to be rid of her. It would seem, however, that his mother was much more afraid of Michael's exposure to the lure of other women and preferred an unalluring wife.

Both women seemed to have forgotten the original cause of their dismay—and in his mother's case, horror—Michael's interest in boys. Only Erna knew of his clandestine relationship with his father but drew no conclusions from it. By now, it was clearer to me that Michael had been used by both his parents to satisfy unacknowledged erotic needs. Escape from the incestuous mother landed him in an exciting conspiracy with his father. This did nothing to alleviate the need to escape his dangerous predilection by flights into heterosexuality which were only one remove from a return to the erotic mother. The strong narcissistic component in the choices, if they can be called choices, perhaps masked the more important element of his sexually undetermined status so that the various roles came easily to him. What could be more mixed up than the role of a seductive mother with a penis approaching his young boy self? Towards his father, he was more like a passive girlish figure having a relationship with father behind a jealous mother's back, yet in his heterosexual relationships he became a ruthless male, all tender feeling being a sham to seduce women.

I had wondered if the father and son would end up living together. It was a possibility as the father then lived almost entirely in a country cottage which the mother never visited. I doubted, however, that either of them would risk making their relationship evident for it would then be defined. It was this fear of being tied down by the definition of roles which had shaken Michael when divorce and the naming of another woman had been suggested. He feared being defined and thus restricted.

Michael's choice of Erna as someone opposite to himself and to his mother gave her a reality which the 'like' people did not have. But without his fantasy image the fascination involved in sexual attraction could not survive, neither could the positive mothering role once Erna had made it clear that she could not stand his unfaithfulness. Then she became taboo as an object of sexual desire and assumed the devouring aspect of the mother.

And what of the 'unlike' son? After the initial horror of having sired an infant as gruesome as his mother's. Michael came to admire his intelligent toddler and failed to understand his difficulty in tolerating the boy's presence for any length of time. Strong feelings of this kind often hide an attraction which it would be inappropriate to express directly.

144

Indirectly, however, it was expressed by the cruel touch rather than the loving one.

The wish to remain young and innocent is an aspect of paedophilia. It is as if the individual is renewed by contact with a young prototype of the self as yet untainted by 'the dirty devices of the world', as the poet Traherne has it. Michael's fear and horror of the corruption of the flesh was omnipresent. As both husband and father he felt old and finished at twenty-eight. The approaching thirties signalled the end of all creative possibilities; thereafter corruption would hasten him towards disgusting death. Such morbid preoccupations could only be banished by erotic activities. The erect penis symbolized vigorous life which was constantly renewed and was indeed eternal. Alas! this renewal could be only transitory: hence its compulsive nature. Compulsive behaviour is always aimed at a once-and-for-all experience which inevitably fails to reassure.

For Michael and his family, a close friendship developed following the dissolution of the marriage. He was much more often at home than before and he actually spent weekends with his family, willingly helping with the house and children, whereas before he did so reluctantly or not at all. His search for the ideal fantasy woman who would save him from himself continued but with increasing doubt as to her existence. This doubt induced anxiety that he would go after boys again and he returned to the psychiatrist whom he had suddenly left in order to get married. His son was taken to a child guidance clinic, because of guilt about his previous treatment of him, and Erna got the support she needed there. Eventually, Michael moved into the house again and lived as a privileged lodger. It made them both feel safer to be together, yet unbound, and the children benefited. The love of children had taken its rightful place in the creation of a caring environment. Occasional sexual intercourse also became possible. Whether this somewhat diluted life would stand up to stress remained to be seen.

Glossary

ARCHETYPES

Jung's name for the dynamic forces in the collective unconscious which represent the underlying tensions experienced in man's struggle for survival. These forces are personified in folklore and myth and are encountered in dreams, and though the imagery varies from culture to culture, the main themes are more or less universally valid. Typical examples are: Oedipus, the divine child (*puer aeternus*), the witch mother (wicked stepmother, phallic mother), the muses, the wise old man, the hero, the ogre, the shadow. Jung describes the archetypes as 'inherited predispositions'.

COLLECTIVE UNCONSCIOUS

According to Jung, the matrix and source of all consciousness. It is a vast store of the common knowledge and experience unconsciously accumulated through the ages by man and his forebears, and available from generation to generation in the form of archetypes, instincts, behaviour patterns and so on. For the individual, the collective unconscious forms the greater part of the total unconscious, the smaller part being his personal unconscious.

COMPENSATORY PSYCHIC PROCESSES

These are unconscious balancing processes in the psyche. For instance, a very small baby who feels utterly impotent may 'create' a fantasy world in which he is omnipotent. In the same way inferior feelings in the individual may be (over-) compensated by pretentious 'superior' behaviour.

EGO

The central government of the conscious mind. Although in our

146

culture stress is often laid on the negative aspects of this concept (egocentric, egotistic), it is basically man's greatest asset in his development as an individual.

EGO-STRENGTH

The ego needs strength in order not to be overwhelmed by the pressure of outer and (often unknown) inner events, such as may happen in mental illness or, more generally, in urges of a distorting kind as in some instances of sexual deviations.

'GOOD ENOUGH'

A term devised by D. W. Winnicott to describe the image of the breast, and later of the mother, which forms in an infant's psyche when there is a preponderance of good over bad feelings in his experience of being fed, held and generally having his needs met by his mother. The image of the 'good enough' mother is an image of the real mother combining both good and bad. It may be contrasted with the image of the idealized and also the denigrated 'too bad' mother, which occurs when the predominance of bad feelings over good is so unbearable that in order to survive the infant splits the bad from the good and thus loses the reality of the experience.

INDIVIDUATION

The aim, in Jungian terms, of analytical procedure: the process of becoming increasingly a person in one's own right—an individual. It is a dynamic, ongoing process which has no time limit other than death or senility. The stronger and more elastic the ego, the better it can relate to the outer and inner world and the better use it can make of the persona and the dynamic elements, the chaos, ambivalences and tensions of the unconscious.

OEDIPAL SITUATION

A stage in the child's development, often accompanied by anxiety, when he wants to 'possess' the parent of the opposite sex and exclude the parent of the same sex. Occasionally, however, the parent desired is of the same sex as the child. This pattern varies in intensity; if unresolved it can hamper later development in sexual and marital relationships. Incestuous feelings and jealousy are always involved.

PERSONA

A Jungian term for the appearance or façade with which the ego interprets or presents itself to the outer world. If the persona is adaptable and in harmony with the individual's inner reality, it acts as a very necessary bridge to outer events and in relationships with others. But if used purely as a protective and defensive cover-up for inner doubts and fears there is a danger that it can rigidify into a mask. The blimp, the pedant, the 'mutton dressed up as lamb'—these are examples of a too rigid identification with a chosen role. The reliability of the persona depends on that of the ego.

PERSONAL UNCONSCIOUS

According to Jung this term describes the repressed and suppressed memories, urges and other contents of the psyche reaching back to earliest infancy, which the individual has, so to speak, 'disposed of'.

PRE-GENITAL

This refers to an historical phase in the growth of an individual and to an early level of development in which sexual fantasy and excitation (conscious or unconscious) is centred upon the mouth, or the anus, or the urethra or—in the phallic phase—upon the strength and sensations connected with the erect penis. All this represents a level of experience prior to the more mature experience of the generative capacities of the genitalia, male or female.

PRIMAL SCENE

A phrase used to describe the fantasies arising in the young child about the sexual relationship between his parents. The meaning of the term has been extended to include the basic human ingredients of the family: mother, father, boy, girl and babies-inside-the-mother together with the outsider—the cynic and critic of the family. The analysis of unconscious fantasies about the primal scene is important for patients troubled in their marital and other relationships.

PROJECTION

A process whereby a person unconsciously uses other people as mirrors or screens upon which to project an image of aspects of himself or of past experiences which he is unaware of. This is a normal process in development, and if the material so projected is recognized by the projector as part of himself and withdrawn, progress is made towards greater personal integration. Understanding of this mirroring process is more difficult the more the person on whom the projection is made resembles the projected image.

PSYCHE

The totality of the inner world of man.

THE SHADOW

Jung's term to describe the potential qualities of a person which he considers as positive or negative yet is largely unconscious of possessing. Because they are unconscious these qualities are undeveloped and unadapted. They are often projected on to other people where their positive or negative aspects are perceived in a distorting way. A typical example of a projected negative shadow is a scapegoat. Integration of shadow material makes for enlargement of personality.

THE 'STUFFING' MOTHER

This describes a mother who forces food, attention, advice, education, even protection on a child according to *her* desires and judgement rather than in response to *his* needs, his spontaneous appetite or his growth processes. This can occur in many realms of life and one of its most important aspects is that it is counter-productive. The 'stuffing mother' may be distinguished from the 'phallic mother' in that the latter represents a child's archetypal fantasy of a mother who possesses a stiff penis (cf. the witch with big nose, chin and broomstick). This fantasy occurs when the actual mother is unusually sharp, penetrative, domineering and pseudo-masculine.